Classic Caribbean Cooking

Classic Caribbean Cooking

Sharon Atkin

H
HANSIB

First published in Great Britain 2001 by Hansib Publications Ltd

Hansib Publications, PO Box 34621, London E17 4GL
Hansib Publications, Orchard Road, Royston, Hertfordshire SG8 5HA

www.hansib-books.com

ISBN 1 870518 58 6

Cover designed by Graphic Resolutions, Hertfordshire

Production by Books of Colour, Hertfordshire

Printed and bound by Interprint Limited, Malta

Contents

Acknowledgements

Since the tender age of seven, I have been cooking, firstly for fun then out of economic necessity. At various times in my life I have been fortunate to travel extensively and I have wanted to recreate the dishes I experienced from many parts of the world. Cooking, for me, has been cathartic as well as therapeutic, and I heartily recommend it.

Throughout my research - both in and out of the Caribbean - I obtained the help and support of many individuals and organisations, without whom this book would never have been possible.

I would like offer heartfelt thanks to the following: the former High Commissioner for Dominica, who gave me so many of the recipes that his sister, Hazel, had researched over years, both in the rural and urban areas of Dominica. I am indebted to both of them; the St Lucia Tourist Board, which gave me recipes and information about the produce, country and the people; the co-owner of the famous 'Butters' Guyanese restaurant in London, Peter Simpson, who provided some of his recipes; the many people from Trinidad, Barbados, Cuba, Guyana and Antigua, and those from the Dutch and French Caribbean, as well as other Caribbean nationals who shared the love of their native cuisine with me, and allowed me to print their special recipes; the many Africans, Indians, Chinese, Arawaks, Arabs, Caribs and Europeans whose sacrifice, sweat, toil and skill, combined to create Caribbean cuisine, which I consider to be the best cuisine in the world.

Thanks are also due to Arif Ali, of Hansib Publications, for commissioning this book and for having faith in my culinary interests and skills; Kash Ali, also of Hansib Publications, for his editing, design and management of the project; Shareef Ali, for designing the cover; Dr Hazel Smith; Aileen Dawson; Sonita Alleyne; TV chef and author, Ainsley Harriott; TV cook and author, Mridula Baljekar, who encouraged me to write the book; the legions of family members and friends, particularly Stephen Bubb, Anthony Vetters and Tim Allen, who have asked me to cater for them and their guests on so many occasions; Brenda Naylor; Chi-Chi Iweajunwa; Tobias Tak; Charles Augins; Tony Levin; Pauline Clarke, Marketing Manager of Enco Products; Galina Panova; Dov, Tamara and Ben Mielnik; Adina Berger and Denise Louther; Ray Warleigh, to whom I dedicate the recipe for rice and peas; Sarah Modebe; Vivienne Rochester; Tom Williams, for whom I will cook at any hour of the day or night; Elorine Grant; Lisa Richards; William and Minnie Louther, my parents-in-law; and all those people over the years, and from around the world, who have eaten my food and, in most cases, have come back for more, time and again!

Special thanks are also due to the members of my family who first gave me Jamaican food. They all pride themselves on their high culinary standards which, in some instances, have won them awards and recommendations for their contribution to livestock, agriculture and hot sauces; to my father, Howard Gray, for his curried lobster, jerk pork and all that he still cooks. His example of endurance and industry was instilled in both my brother and I; to his late mother and sisters, Aunt Clare, Aunt Irma and Aunt Hyacinth, who have all fed me well, in particular, my late Aunt Florrie who was also my godmother and who taught me so much about cooking. She was the greatest untrained chef that I have ever known who maintained that it was her father's sister, Aunt Ros, who was her inspiration and mentor. There was never a time when she was not prepared to feed people who would drop by unexpectedly. Food was always available in copious quantities and devoured with relish; to Aunt Dathlyn, who lost her sight many years ago, and lives on her own, and still manages to cook wonderful food; to my brother, Orlando (Landy), his wife, Claudette, and his seven children, Jawara, Kenyatta, Abena, Afiya, Al Hadji, Ama and Aleema, who all love to eat. From them, and for them, Rastafarian cooking is something that I learnt about, and I included many recipes with them, and Rastafarian friends, in mind; to my son, Neil, whose love of ackee and saltfish, rice and peas and any fish dish, links him to his Caribbean ancestry and culture; to my grandson, Ellis, who spends many hours in the kitchen 'helping' me with the cooking, and his sister, Kaylie.

Since completing this book, three of my dearest friends are no longer with us. Leonie Urdang, Dr Dora Boatemah and Hassia Levy-Agron gave me support and encouragement, and in the case of Leonie and Dora, sampled many dishes. They are sadly missed.

And, finally, I would like to thank my late husband, William (Bill) Louther, who supported and encouraged me throughout the research and writing of this book, but most of all for his love and faith in me. His death on 7 May 1998 robbed the world of a great dancer/choreographer, teacher and humanitarian, and a loving husband. This book is dedicated to his memory.

Sharon Atkin Louther
October 2001

Introduction

This book is a celebration of the ingenuity and creativity of the people of the Caribbean - from the original Amerindian tribes, to the African, European, Asian and Middle Eastern settlers. Over the centuries, they have created a unique cuisine that owes much to various parts of the world as well as to the Caribbean as a whole.

For more than four hundred years following the arrival of Christopher Columbus, the Caribbean region experienced turbulent power struggles between various European colonisers. Each nation brought its own customs and ways of life which had a profound influence on the region.

The first people to arrive in significant numbers were Africans captured as slaves from the west coast of Africa. They were followed by indentured Indian and Chinese labourers, and Middle Eastern traders. All of these settlers made their mark on the Caribbean in what has become a unique melting pot of cultures and traditions.

In Britain, during the economic conditions of the post-war boom, labour from the Caribbean was eagerly sought, especially for the newly-established National Health Service and for public transport. Caribbean communities rapidly developed in many parts of London as well as in other major cities, and with this growth came the rise in demand for Caribbean produce.

As a child growing up in Britain, I looked forward to the meals that were prepared in the traditional Caribbean way. And although typical Caribbean ingredients, such as breadfruit, cassava, yams, mangoes, saltfish and red snapper, were not as readily available as they are today, my grandmother would always maintain our links with the Caribbean by sending cakes, fruits and coconuts, usually at Christmas time.

The recipes in this book have been gathered from throughout the Caribbean. In some cases, where the ingredients to certain recipes may be difficult to obtain, I have included an appropriate substitute. A comprehensive glossary is also included, particularly because some countries have their own names for the same types of food.

Many of the historic recipes are cooked in one pot - whether on a stove or in the oven - as it has been done for centuries throughout the Caribbean. This method of cooking survives to date, and the traditional Dutch oven, which is a large pot, is ideal for this type of cooking.

As general rule, I have used extra virgin olive oil in many recipes, simply because it is purer and made from the first cold pressing of the olives. It is also healthier and has a better flavour for salad dressings. For frying, however, a groundnut or sunflower oil is perfectly suitable, unless the recipe states otherwise.

Many of the recipes are made using unsalted butter, but if you prefer, a good quality margarine is an acceptable substitute. When cooking the Indo-Caribbean dishes, ghee is the authentic ingredient but, if preferred, sunflower oil or unsalted butter mixed with a small amount of cooking oil may be used.

I prefer to use fresh herbs but sometimes it may be difficult to obtain them. By all means, use the dried variety but remember that dried herbs have a more concentrated flavour, so it is necessary to reduce the quantity.

Cooking is as much about personal taste as it is about technique, and these recipes can serve as guides for the more experienced or adventurous cook. By adopting this attitude, you will be able to create your own variations on these original themes, in much the same way that Caribbean cuisine drew from international variations and influences.

With more than three hundred recipes, catering for almost every type of diet, Classic Caribbean Cooking is a book for everyone - no matter what their culinary skills. All that remains is for you to roll up your sleeves and start cooking classic Caribbean food!

Sharon Atkin Louther

Chicken

Alicot

Jamaica

Ingredients
680 g/1½ lb chicken giblets
300 ml/10 fl oz vegetable or chicken stock
2 onions, finely chopped
2 rashers streaky bacon, diced
1 teaspoon tomato puree
1 scotch bonnet pepper, de-seeded, sliced
1 sprig thyme
1 bay leaf
Cooking oil
Salt and freshly ground black pepper

Method
Cut the giblets into bite-size pieces then brown in the cooking oil in a deep frying pan. Remove and discard giblets and add the bacon, thyme, bay leaf, tomato puree, onions and scotch bonnet pepper and sauté for a few minutes. Add the stock, bring to the boil and simmer for 1 hour. Season and remove thyme and bay leaf before serving.

Serving suggestion
Serve hot with boiled yam and a green vegetable.

Serves 4

Asopao de Pollo

Puerto Rico

Ingredients

1.3 kg/3 lb chicken pieces
1.5 litres/2½ pints chicken stock
2 tablespoons drained capers
12 stuffed green olives
4 tablespoons tomato paste
2 teaspoons white wine vinegar
340 g/12 oz easy cook long grain white rice
½ teaspoon paprika
3 teaspoons extra virgin olive oil
300 ml/10 fl oz sofrito (see page 294)
3 teaspoons fresh sage, finely chopped
3 teaspoons salt

Method

Mix the garlic, salt, paprika, olive oil, vinegar and sage, then rub the mixture into the chicken pieces and leave for 1 hour. Place sofrito, olives, capers, tomato paste and chicken in a large saucepan, cover and simmer on a low heat for 15 minutes. Add the stock and bring to the boil. Add the rice, reduce heat and cook for 15 minutes or until liquid is absorbed.

Serving suggestion

Serve hot with cooked petite pois and garnished with raw capsicums.

Serves 5 to 6

Barbecued Chicken

St Vincent

Ingredients
1.8 kg/4 lb roasting chicken, boned and skinned
230 g/8 oz pitted green olives
150 g/5 fl oz strawberry syrup
900 g/2 lb butter
1 teaspoon black pepper
1 teaspoon powdered ginger
½ teaspoon saltpetre (see Author's note)

Method
Cut the chicken into 5 cm/2 inch pieces and pat dry with kitchen paper. Season the chicken with salt, pepper, ginger and saltpetre. Thread the chicken pieces and olives onto skewers, preferably metal ones. Melt butter and syrup, and keep mixture warm, and brush chicken and olive skewers frequently while cooking on the barbecue. Cook until chicken is golden outside and the juices run clear.

Serves 6 to 8

Author's note: Saltpetre is often available from pharmacists and acts as a preserving agent.

Chicken and Sweet Potato Casserole

Guyana

Ingredients
450 g/1 lb chicken pieces
340 g/12 oz sweet potatoes
180 ml/6 fl oz coconut milk
2 tablespoons poultry marinade (see page 286)
1.2 litres/2 pints corn oil or groundnut oil
1 clove garlic
1 tablespoon light soy sauce
1 tablespoon cornflour
2 teaspoons white sugar
4 slices fresh ginger
1 teaspoon salt

Sauce
2 teaspoons chicken stock powder or ½ chicken stock cube
1 tablespoon light soy sauce
340 ml/12 fl oz water

Method
Wash and dry the chicken, cut into bite-size pieces and place in a bowl for 20 minutes with the poultry marinade. Cut sweet potato into ½ inch slices. Shred ginger and chop garlic. Mix coconut milk with sugar and salt. Heat the oil to boiling point in a deep fat fryer or wok, and fry potato until golden, remove and place in a casserole, then fry the chicken pieces until brown and remove to the casserole, place on top of potato. Stir fry garlic and ginger in a tablespoon of oil for 2 minutes, then

transfer to casserole along with the sauce ingredients, cover and bring to the boil, then reduce the heat and simmer for 30 minutes or until cooked. Add coconut mixture, heat through but do not boil. Serve hot.

Serving suggestion
Serve with corn on the cob and spinach.

Serves 4 to 5

Classic Caribbean Cooking

Chicken Curry

Guadeloupe

Ingredients
1.3 kg/3 lb chicken pieces
150 ml/5 fl oz chicken stock
3 medium onions, finely chopped
3 large carrots, peeled, thinly sliced
3 cloves garlic, finely chopped
1 hot red pepper, de-seeded
60 g/2 oz chickpeas, soaked overnight in cold water
2 tablespoons parsley, finely chopped
2 sprigs thyme
3 tablespoons curry powder
1 teaspoon ground pimento (allspice)
1 tablespoon white wine vinegar
3 teaspoons salt
600 ml/1 pint cold water

Method
Drain the chickpeas then rinse twice in cold water. Heat the oil in a large saucepan or casserole and, over a high heat, brown the chicken. Next, sauté onions and garlic until both are soft. Add all the ingredients except the carrots. Bring to the boil and cook covered for 45 minutes over a low heat. Finally, add the carrots and cook until both peas and carrots are tender.

Serving suggestion
Serve hot with rice.

Serves 6 to 8

Chicken Fricassee

Dominica

Ingredients
1.3 kg/3 lb roasting chicken, jointed
1 medium onion, chopped
1 clove garlic, crushed
2 sprigs thyme
2 tablespoons malt vinegar
1 tablespoon tomato ketchup
1 dash Worcestershire sauce
1 tablespoon sugar
Salt and pepper to taste
Cooking oil

Method
Clean the chicken and dry thoroughly. Season with salt and pepper, chopped onion, thyme, garlic and a tablespoon of vinegar and leave for at least 2 hours. Heat 3 tablespoons of oil with the sugar in a heavy casserole until the sugar melts. Coat the chicken in the melted sugar and oil and brown until nicely crisp. Add the remainder of the ingredients and a little water, and cook for 30 to 40 minutes until tender.

Serving suggestion
Serve with rice, yam or fried plantain and a salad.

Serves 4 as a main course

Chicken with Pineapple

Cuba

Ingredients

8 chicken quarters
3 large tomatoes, skinned and chopped
1 ripe pineapple, peeled, cored and chopped
4 tablespoons lemon juice, freshly squeezed
1 onion, minced
2 tablespoons unsalted butter
3 tablespoons currants
1 teaspoon finely grated lemon peel
2 teaspoons brown sugar
1 tablespoon light rum
Plain flour
Salt and freshly ground black pepper

Method

Brush the chicken with lemon juice, season with salt and pepper, and dust with flour. Heat the butter in a frying pan and brown the chicken. Add the onions, tomatoes and lemon peel, and cook on a low heat until chicken is tender, about 30 minutes. Add the currants, brown sugar and some more salt and pepper and cook for a further 10 minutes. Place chopped pineapple in a processor or blender and blend to a smooth puree. Transfer to a small pan, heat and simmer until the sauce has reduced and thickened, then add the rum and serve hot with the chicken.

Serving suggestion

Serve with plain boiled rice

Serves 8

Fried Chicken Legs

Trinidad

Ingredients
8 chicken drumsticks
2 tablespoons soy sauce
2 tablespoons arrowroot
1 tablespoon sherry
1 tablespoon finely chopped spring onion
450 ml/15 fl oz cooking oil
2 teaspoons freshly ground black pepper

Method
Chop the chicken legs into three pieces and place in a bowl with the soy sauce, sherry and pepper. Leave to marinate for at least 20 minutes, turning occasionally. Drain then coat the chicken with cornflour or arrowroot. Heat the oil in a large wok or deep fat fryer. Add a few pieces of chicken at a time to the hot oil, lower the heat, and cook until chicken is golden brown on the outside and cooked through, about 15 minutes. In a small frying pan take one tablespoon of the oil and stir-fry the spring onion for 2 minutes over a moderate heat and garnish the chicken. Serve hot.

Serving suggestion
Serve with fried rice or chow mein.

Serves 4

Jellied Chicken

Martinique

Ingredients
1.3 kg/3 lb chicken
2 eggs, hard boiled and quartered
1 onion, peeled and studded with 6 cloves
2 tablespoons lemon juice
1 tablespoon Worcestershire sauce
1 teaspoon pepper sauce
2 sprigs thyme
2 sprigs parsley
1 bay leaf
30 g/1 oz gelatine
Salt and freshly ground white pepper

Method
Cover chicken with cold water in a large pot, add thyme, parsley, onion, bay leaf, salt and pepper. Bring to the boil then cover and simmer until chicken is tender, about 40 minutes. Remove the chicken and leave to cool, then boil the stock rapidly until about 1.2 litres/2 pints of liquid remains. Remove from the heat and strain, then stir in the lemon juice, Worcestershire sauce, pepper sauce and gelatine, and leave to cool. Meanwhile, shred the chicken, and then add to a wetted mould with the eggs and pour over the gelatine mixture. Leave to set for about an hour. Turn out and serve.

Serving suggestion
Serve as a starter or with other salads as a main course.

Serves 4 as a starter or 6 as part of a main course

Pickled Chicken

Cuba

Ingredients
1.8 kg/4 lb roasting chicken cut into portions
4 medium onions, thinly sliced
5 cloves garlic, chopped
1 hot green pepper
2 fresh bay leaves
1½ teaspoons fresh oregano
300 ml/10 fl oz extra virgin olive oil
150 ml/5 fl oz white wine vinegar
Salt and freshly ground black pepper

Method
Season the chicken joints with salt and pepper and place in a
Dutch oven with the onions, garlic, hot pepper, bay leaves and
oregano. Next, pour oil and vinegar over the chicken and
simmer for 30 to 40 minutes or until chicken is tender. Discard
bay leaves and hot pepper and refrigerate when cold.

Serving suggestion
Serve cold with a green salad containing stuffed green olives.

Serves 6

Poulet au Lait de Coco

Haiti

Ingredients
1.3 kg/3 lb chicken pieces
2 large onions, finely chopped
360 ml/12 fl oz coconut milk
90 ml/3 fl oz chicken stock
1 bouquet garni (see Glossary)
1 tablespoon curry powder
3 tablespoons unsalted butter
1 teaspoon freshly ground salt and pepper

Method
Melt the butter in a large deep frying pan and sauté the chicken pieces and onion until both are golden brown. Then stir in the curry powder and cook for further two minutes. Add the stock, bouquet garni, coconut milk and salt and pepper. Bring to the boil, cover and simmer for about 30 minutes or until chicken is tender and the sauce has reduced by about a third. Serve hot.

Serving suggestion
Serve with boiled rice and a green salad or boiled vegetables.

Serves 5 to 6

Beef

Beef Curry

Trinidad and Tobago

Ingredients
1.3 kg/3 lb lean braising steak, cubed
450 ml/15 fl oz coconut milk
3 medium onions, finely chopped
1 fresh hot red pepper, de-seeded and finely chopped
3 cloves garlic, finely chopped
2 tablespoons curry powder
1½ tablespoons finely grated ginger
Freshly ground black pepper
Salt

Method
Heat some cooking oil in a large cast iron casserole or Dutch oven, then add the onions, garlic, ginger and curry powder. Stir over a medium heat for 1 minute to soften onion and combine the flavours. Add the cubed meat and mix well with the seasonings. Cook for about 3 minutes then add the coconut milk, hot pepper, salt and black pepper. Cover and simmer for 1½ hours or until meat is tender.

Serving suggestion
Serve hot with plain boiled rice, plain roti and mango chutney.

Serves 6

Beef Hash

Puerto Rico

Ingredients
900 g/2 lb minced steak
3 large tomatoes, skinned and chopped
3 spring onions, chopped
1 large red capsicum
1 hot red pepper, de-seeded and chopped
2 tablespoons stuffed green olives (stuffed with pimentos)
1 clove garlic, finely chopped
110 g/4 oz seedless raisins
Freshly ground black pepper
Salt

Method
Heat some cooking oil in a large deep frying pan and add the spring onions, garlic and peppers. Cook for 2 minutes over a moderate heat or until the spring onions have softened, but not browned. Next, add the meat and cook briskly until it is broken up and has browned. Add the tomatoes, raisins, salt and pepper and simmer uncovered for 25 minutes or until cooked. Add the olives for the last 2 minutes of cooking time.

Serving suggestion
Serve hot with plain boiled rice, or creamed yam, or creamed sweet potatoes.

Serves 5 to 6

Bolonger Beef

Guyana

Ingredients
1.3 kg/3 lb braising steak
450 g/1 lb medium tomatoes, skinned and chopped
3 medium aubergines, peeled and diced
2 medium onions, sliced
2 cloves garlic, crushed
2 sprigs thyme
Cooking oil
60 ml/2 fl oz water
Freshly ground black pepper
Salt

Method
Season the meat with salt and pepper, then cut into cubes. Lightly sauté in cooking oil in a frying pan, then transfer to a large pot. Add all the other ingredients and pour in the water. Season to taste and cook on a low heat for about 2 hours or until meat is tender and tomatoes and aubergines have combined to produce a rich sauce.

Serving suggestion
Serve with plain boiled rice or boiled potatoes.

Serves 4 to 6

Corned Beef

Jamaica

Ingredients
1.3 kg/3 lb silverside beef
4 slices green scotch bonnet pepper
3 spring onions
14 pimento (allspice) berries
2 cloves garlic
3 teaspoons fresh thyme leaves
3 tablespoons salt
3 teaspoons freshly ground black pepper
½ teaspoon saltpetre

Method
Blend the pimento berries, spring onions, scotch bonnet peppers, black pepper and garlic into a smooth puree. Add the thyme, salt and saltpetre and mix well. Make some incisions in the meat and stuff most of the seasoning paste into the slits and cover the rest of the meat with the remaining paste. Place meat in an enamel or earthenware dish and cover tightly with tin foil or clear film. Refrigerate for 4 days, remembering to turn the meat daily. When the meat is ready to cook, place it in a large pot and cover with water. Bring to the boil, then turn down the heat and simmer for about 2 hours or until the meat is tender (take care not to allow the meat to break up).

Serving suggestion
Serve hot with salad and rice, or mustard pickles and chutney. Serve cold in sandwiches. Serve fried with potatoes, sweet peppers and tomatoes.

Serves 4 to 5 as a main course

Curried Veal

Jamaica

Ingredients

900 g/2 lb stewing veal, diced
600 ml/1 pint chicken or veal stock
230 g/8 oz celery, finely chopped
2 medium onions, finely chopped
1 eating apple, finely chopped
½ green scotch bonnet pepper, de-seeded and sliced
2 eggs, size 2, well beaten
110 g/4 oz unsalted butter
4 tablespoons molasses
1 tablespoon tomato puree
2 tablespoons curry powder
½ teaspoon ground ginger
1 dash hot pepper sauce
1 teaspoon freshly ground black pepper
1 teaspoon salt

Method

Heat the butter in a Dutch oven or cast iron casserole. Brown onions lightly and remove. In the same pot, brown the veal then remove and keep warm. Fry curry powder in the pot until brown but not burnt, then return the meat and onions, along with the remainder of the ingredients, except the eggs. Simmer until the meat is tender, about 40 minutes. Stir occasionally and make sure that the liquid does not evaporate too much. Add more water or stock if required. Two minutes before the end of cooking, stir in the beaten eggs and serve.

Serving suggestion

Serve with rice, fried green bananas or mango chutney, and salad.

Serves 6 to 8

Pan Fried Liver

Dominica

Ingredients
450 g/1 lb ox liver
1 large onion, sliced
1 clove garlic, crushed
2 tablespoon oil
1 tablespoon butter
1 teaspoon vinegar

Method
Place liver in boiling water for 2 minutes, then take out and remove the thin skin, then cut liver into cubes. Heat the oil in a heavy pot, add butter, onions, garlic, vinegar and liver. Sauté for 2 minutes. Add a little water, about 60 ml/2 fl oz, then cover and simmer for 15 minutes.

Serves 2

Author's note: Pig's, calf's or lamb's liver may also be used as an alternative, although many consider that ox liver has the best flavour.

Pot Roast Beef

Jamaica

Ingredients
1.8 kg/4 lb topside or silverside beef
600 ml/1 pint beef stock
230 g/8 oz potatoes, peeled and diced
230 g/8 oz yellow yam, peeled and diced
3 carrots, peeled and sliced
3 spring onions, finely chopped
2 green scotch bonnet peppers
1 large tomato, finely chopped
1 medium onion, finely chopped
3 cloves garlic, finely chopped
3 sprigs fresh thyme, finely chopped
3 sprigs fresh parsley, finely chopped
4 teaspoons dark brown sugar
2 tablespoons dark malt vinegar
2 tablespoons dark soy sauce
Freshly ground black pepper
Salt

Method
Finely chop one of the scotch bonnet peppers and mix well with the tomato, spring onions, garlic, parsley and thyme to create a seasoning mixture. Cut fairly deep slits all over the meat, then stuff with the seasoning, rubbing any excess over the meat. Place in a deep dish, pour over vinegar and soy sauce and leave at room temperature for 4 hours, basting frequently. Then drain the meat, pat dry and rub in the sugar. Brown the meat in a casserole or cast iron pot, add the stock, onion, scotch bonnet pepper, and left-over marinade. Bring to the boil, then cover and simmer for 3 hours or until meat is tender.

Add carrots, yam and potatoes for the last 20 minutes of cooking time. When cooked, remove the meat from the pot and prepare a sauce using the remaining juice by thickening with 2-3 teaspoons of arrowroot mixed with cold water. Remove pepper before serving.

Serving suggestion

Serve with vegetables and rice and peas, or plain boiled rice.

Serves 4 to 6

Red Stripe Stew

Jamaica

Ingredients
1.3 kg/3 lb braising steak, cubed
2 large cans Red Stripe lager (or similar)
1 medium onion, finely chopped
2 cloves garlic, peeled and finely chopped
2 sprigs thyme
2 bay leaves
1 tablespoon tomato puree
Cooking oil for frying
Freshly ground black pepper
Salt

Method
Season the braising steak with salt and pepper. Heat the oil in a large casserole or Dutch oven, add the onion and cook until softened, then add the meat. Brown the meat then add the garlic and sauté for 1 minute. Add the remainder of the ingredients, bring to the boil, cover and simmer for 2½ hours. When the meat is cooked, add a tablespoon of cornflour mixed with cold water, to thicken the sauce.

Serving suggestion
Serve hot with boiled yam and plain boiled rice, or rice and peas and buttered cabbage.

Serves 6

Ropa Vieja
Dominican Republic

Ingredients
900 g/2 lb left-over beef
2 large onions, finely chopped
2 large tomatoes, peeled and chopped
1 hot red pepper, de-seeded and finely chopped
1 green capsicum, de-seeded and finely chopped
3 cloves garlic, finely chopped
3 tablespoons tomato puree
½ tablespoon drained capers
1 tablespoon fresh coriander, finely chopped
3 teaspoons fresh oregano, finely chopped
3 tablespoons cooking oil
1 teaspoon sugar

Method
Heat cooking oil in a large frying pan or Dutch oven over a medium heat and then sauté the onion, garlic and capsicum until soft but not browned. Add capers, tomatoes and tomato paste and cook for a minute then add oregano, sugar, coriander, meat and hot pepper and cook for 10 minutes over a low heat.

Serving suggestion
Serve hot with plain boiled rice or rice and peas and fried plantain.

Serves 5 to 6

Rum Steak

Haiti

Ingredients
1.3 kg/3 lb sirloin steak
2 tablespoons dark rum
2 tablespoons claret
1 heaped tablespoon black peppercorns, crushed
2 tablespoons beef consommé (see Glossary)
2 tablespoons unsalted butter

Method
Cut the steak into 6 portions and tenderise. Coat both sides of each steak with the crushed peppercorns. Stand at room temperature for 30 minutes. Combine wine and consommé and set aside. Heat butter in a cast iron frying pan and fry the steak briskly over a high heat for 2 minutes, then pour on rum and set alight. Shake pan carefully until flames are out, then add wine and consommé mixture. Heat and serve when steak is cooked to your own preference.

Serving suggestion
This rich dish only requires a simple accompaniment such as boiled parsley potatoes, creamed potatoes, or boiled white rice with steamed vegetables or a green salad.

Serves 6

Spiced Beef

Martinique

Ingredients
900 g/2 lb braising steak, cubed
2 limes, freshly squeezed
1 hot red pepper, de-seeded and chopped
4 cloves garlic, crushed
2 teaspoons freshly grated ginger
4 ground cloves
3 fresh bay leaves
1 tablespoon dark rum
2 teaspoons annatto liquid
3 tablespoons unsalted butter
Freshly ground black pepper
Salt

Method
Mix the lime juice, hot pepper, ginger, cloves, garlic and 2 teaspoons salt to create a marinade. Place in a bowl with the meat and mix well. Cover and leave in the refrigerator for 2 days. Then drain and reserve the marinade. In a cast iron pot or Dutch oven, melt the butter and sauté the meat for about 10 minutes or until well browned. Add the reserved marinade and the rest of the ingredients and simmer on a low heat for 2 to 2½ hours or until the meat is tender, stirring occasionally. Serve hot.

Serving suggestion
Serve with creamed yams, boiled rice, or boiled potatoes and a green salad or steamed cabbage.

Serves 4 to 6

Lamb
& Goat

Curried Goat

Jamaica

Ingredients

1.3 kg/3 lb goat meat, chopped
600 ml/1 pint chicken or lamb stock
110 g/4 oz creamed coconut, or 1 can coconut milk
3 large onions, chopped

1 green scotch bonnet pepper
4 pimento berries
1 clove garlic, chopped
4 tablespoons hot curry powder
Salt and freshly ground black pepper

Method

Mix the goat meat together with the onion, salt, pepper and 2 tablespoons of curry powder. Do this by hand and then leave overnight in a cool place. Next day, heat some cooking oil in a large frying pan and briskly fry the meat (without the onion) until browned, then transfer to a large cast iron pot or casserole. Add pimento, stock, remaining curry powder and scotch bonnet pepper to the pot. Sauté the onions until golden, then add to the pot, bring to the boil, then simmer for about 2½ hours or until meat is tender. Add coconut and garlic (and more curry powder if required) and cook for another 15 minutes.

Serving suggestion

Serve hot with plain boiled rice, mango chutney and boiled green bananas.

Serves 6

Author's note: Some cooks like to add diced potatoes during the last 20 minutes of cooking time. This adds texture, flavour and thickens the sauce.

Goat Water

Montserrat

Ingredients
1.3 kg/3 lb goat, leg or shoulder, cubed
1 hot pepper, de-seeded
1 clove garlic, crushed
3 cloves
30 g/1 oz butter
30 g/1 oz plain flour
1 tablespoon tomato puree
Salt and freshly ground black pepper

Method
Put all the ingredients, except the flour, in a large pot and cover with cold water. Bring to the boil, then cover and simmer for 2 to 3 hours, or until meat is tender. Make a thin paste with the flour and water, add to the pot and simmer until the stew has thickened.

Serving suggestion
Serve hot with boiled rice and dasheen.

Serves 6 to 8

Jellied Lamb

Grenada

Ingredients
230 g/8 oz roasted lamb, diced
1 lettuce
110 g/4 oz white cabbage, finely shredded
1 tablespoon cooked green peas
2 tablespoons white wine vinegar
2 teaspoons freshly squeezed lime juice
10 g/½ oz dried gelatine
2 teaspoons sugar
1 teaspoon salt
Grated nutmeg
600 ml/1 pint water

Method
Dissolve the gelatine over a pan of hot water, add the lime juice, vinegar and salt, strain into a bowl and leave to cool. Meanwhile, place the lamb, half the shredded lettuce, cabbage, peas and nutmeg into a wetted mould. Add the gelatine and place in the refrigerator until set.

Serving suggestion
Serve on a bed of the remaining shredded lettuce as a starter or light lunch.

Serves 4

Lamchi

Aruba

Ingredients

900 g/2 lb lamb, cut into 5 cm/2 inch cubes
8 slices streaky bacon, halved
4 onions, quartered
4 tomatoes, quartered
1 green capsicum, de-seeded
2 tablespoons grated onion
1 clove garlic, crushed
6 slices fresh pineapple, halved
Juice of 4 limes
3 tablespoons extra virgin olive oil
1 tablespoon chilli powder
3 teaspoons curry powder
2 teaspoons ground ginger
2 teaspoons ground turmeric
1 teaspoon salt

Method

Mix the lamb, ginger, olive oil, garlic, salt, chilli powder, turmeric, and grated onion, and leave to marinate in the refrigerator overnight. Next day, thread the meat cubes onto long skewers, alternating with onion, tomato, pineapple and bacon wrapped round capsicum, thus creating a kebab. Grill on a moderate to high heat for 15 to 20 minutes, turning frequently to ensure that the kebabs are thoroughly cooked and evenly browned.

Serving suggestion

Serve hot with peanut sauce and boiled rice.

Serves 4

Author's note: If metal skewers are not available, use wooden ones soaked in cold water for at least two hours. This limits burning the wood and also allows the meat to be removed easily.

Meat Stew

Curaçao

Ingredients

900 g/2 lb leg of kid/goat
230 g/8 oz salt beef
4 old potatoes, peeled and diced
4 small tomatoes, skinned and chopped
2 hot red peppers, de-seeded and finely chopped
1 green capsicum, de-seeded and chopped
1 large onion, finely chopped
3 cloves garlic, crushed
3 tablespoons annatto oil
3 tablespoons cooking oil
1 tablespoon fresh lime juice
Freshly ground black pepper

Method

Soak salt beef in water for 1 hour, using enough water to completely cover. Meanwhile, cut kid/goat meat off the bone and cut into cubes. Drain beef then cut into cubes, fry in a little oil together with the kid until brown. Place in a large saucepan and cover with cold water and bring to the boil, then simmer for 1¼ hours. When meat is tender, strain and reserve the stock. Heat oil in a large saucepan or Dutch oven, add onions and peppers, and sauté over a medium heat until onion is tender, but not brown. Next, add the garlic and sauté for 1 minute. Add meat, annatto oil, tomatoes, lime juice and black pepper, and simmer for 20 minutes. Add stock and then the potatoes and bring to the boil, then cover and simmer for 40 minutes or until potatoes are cooked.

Serving suggestion

This should be served hot and provides a complete meal. However, it may also be served with plain boiled rice.

Serves 5 to 6

Roast Lamb

Martinique

Ingredients
1.8 kg/4 lb leg lamb
3 cloves garlic, peeled
3 teaspoons freshly chopped rosemary
2 teaspoons chopped parsley
2 teaspoons fresh oregano
2 teaspoons freshly chopped coriander
3 teaspoons freshly ground black pepper
1 teaspoon freshly ground sea salt

Method
Trim off excess fat from the leg of lamb, then cut about 10 or 12 slits into the meat. Thoroughly mix together all the ingredients and stuff the mixture into the slits and then leave covered in the refrigerator for 24 hours. Roast the prepared meat at gas mark 5, 375°F, 190°C for 2 - 2½ hours.

Serves 4 to 6

Serving suggestion
Serve with roast breadfruit, roast potatoes, sautéed carrots and callaloo or with a selection of your favourite vegetables.

Seasoned Lamb

Guadeloupe

Ingredients
900 g/2 lb lean lamb, cubed
300 ml/10 fl oz lamb stock
300 ml/10 fl oz coconut milk
3 large tomatoes, peeled and chopped
2 medium onions, finely chopped
4 cloves garlic, finely chopped
3 tablespoons single cream
3 tablespoons freshly squeezed lime juice
80 g/3 oz unsalted butter
2 sprigs fresh thyme
2 whole cloves
½ teaspoon ground coriander
¼ teaspoon freshly grated nutmeg
¼ teaspoon ground cinnamon
Salt and freshly ground black pepper

Method
Heat the butter in a large cast iron pot or Dutch oven, add the cubed lamb and onions and sauté for a couple of minutes. Next, add the tomatoes, nutmeg, cinnamon, garlic, cloves, thyme, salt and pepper and cook for 5 minutes before adding the stock and coconut milk. Cover and then simmer for about 2½ hours, then add the cream and cook for another 5 minutes, then add the lime and cook for another minute.

Serving suggestion
Serve hot with rice and a green vegetable or buttered carrots.

Serves 4

Classic Caribbean Cookery

Pork

Baked Pork

Jamaica

Ingredients
1.8 kg/4 lbs pork chops
230 g/8 oz tomato puree
3 sticks celery, diced
2 tablespoons brown sugar
1 teaspoon dry mustard
Juice of half a lime
Salt and pepper to taste
150 ml/5 fl oz water

Method
Mix together the tomato puree, celery, lime juice, mustard, brown sugar, salt and pepper to create a sauce. Brown the chops in butter and cooking oil, and transfer to an oven-proof dish. Pour the sauce over the chops and cook in the oven at gas mark 3, 325°F, 160°C, for 2 hours, or until pork is tender.

Serving suggestion
Serve with rice or potatoes or boiled yam and a green vegetable.

Serves 8 to 10

Bami

Surinam

Ingredients

230 g/8 oz pork, cubed
110 g/4 oz dried shrimps
230 g/8 oz rice noodles, cooked as instructed
110 g/4 oz fresh washed bean sprouts
110 g/4 oz white cabbage, finely sliced
1 large onion, finely chopped
1 leek, washed and thinly sliced
2 hot peppers, de-seeded and finely chopped
3 spring onions, finely chopped
3 cloves garlic
3 tablespoons dark thick soy sauce
1 teaspoon white sugar
½ teaspoon trasi (dried shrimp paste)
60 ml/2 fl oz groundnut oil

Method

Soak dried shrimps in cold water for 2 hours. In a wok or cast iron frying pan, heat 60 ml/2 fl oz of groundnut oil to smoking-point, then stir-fry the pork for 2 minutes or until well brown, then add the shrimps, followed by the onion, garlic, trasi and peppers, and stir-fry for another two minutes or until the onion is clear. Then add the cabbage, bean sprouts, sugar and soy sauce and stir-fry on a medium heat for another minute. Finally, mix in the noodles and fry for a further 2 minutes, stirring constantly.

Serving suggestion

Serve garnished with hard boiled egg, slices of tomato and slices of cucumber.

Serves 4 to 5

Author's note: Trasi is available from Chinese food shops.

Chinese Barbecued Spare Ribs

Jamaica

Ingredients
1.3 kg/3 lbs spare ribs
1 medium onion, chopped
3 stalks celery, diced
3 tablespoons plain flour
½ teaspoon dried mustard
¼ teaspoon paprika
150 ml/5 fl oz hot sauce
150 ml/5 fl oz soy sauce
2 tablespoons white vinegar
2 tablespoons sugar
1 teaspoon salt
2 tablespoons cooking oil
300 ml/10 fl oz water

Method
Mix flour and salt together and rub over spare ribs. Heat oil in a pan and brown the meat, then transfer to a casserole. Brown the onion in remaining fat, then add the rest of the ingredients and bring to the boil. Pour over spare ribs and bake at gas mark 4, 350°F, 180°C, for 1 hour or until tender.

Serving suggestion
Serve with fried or plain rice and straw mushrooms in sesame seed and chilli oil.

Serves 6

Garlic Pork

Guyana

Ingredients
2.7 kg/6 lbs lean leg of pork, boned and cubed
1.2 litres/2 pints malt vinegar
3 small hot red peppers
6 cloves garlic
6 cloves
1 bunch fresh thyme
1 tablespoon salt

Method
Place the cubed pork into a large jar or pot. Using a food processor or pestle and mortar, crush the garlic, thyme and peppers and mix with vinegar, salt and cloves. Pour the mixture over the pork, cover and seal the container and leave to marinate in a cool place for at least a week, longer if possible. After the marinating period, pour the contents of the jar or pot into a frying pan and boil until the vinegar has evaporated. During this process, the pork fat will melt leaving enough oil to fry the pieces of meat. Fry until the pork is brown and crisp at the edges.

Serving suggestion
Serve as part of a festive breakfast.

Serves 6 to 8

Glazed Pork

Trinidad and Tobago

Ingredients
1.8 kg/4 lbs pork fillet
1 hot red pepper, de-seeded and finely chopped
110 g/4 oz garlic, finely chopped
2 teaspoons chopped fresh thyme
450 ml/15 fl oz white wine vinegar
Juice of 1 large lime
1½ teaspoons salt
Freshly ground black pepper
Cooking oil for frying

Method
Cut pork into bite-size pieces and cover with lime juice. Mix all the remaining ingredients together and pour over the meat. Cover and leave to marinate in the refrigerator for 2 days. After marinating, drain the meat on kitchen paper then deep fry in oil until golden brown and well cooked, about 7 minutes.

Serving suggestion
Serve hot with fried sweet potatoes and a green salad.

Serves 6 to 7

Grapefruit Ham

Barbados

Ingredients
1 hock bacon or gammon
1 grapefruit
150 ml/5 fl oz grapefruit juice
20 cloves
Brown sugar
Cinnamon

Method
Soak the bacon in water overnight. After soaking, place in a large pot, cover with fresh cold water then par boil (20 minutes per 450 g/1 lb). Then drain the bacon, cut off the rind and fat, place in a roasting tin and stud the meat with the cloves. Pour grapefruit juice over the bacon and cook in a pre-heated oven at gas mark 4, 350°F, 180°C, for 30 minutes, basting frequently. Peel the grapefruit, remove pith and separate into segments, then dip into a mixture of sugar and cinnamon and brown under a hot grill for a few minutes and serve with slices of cooked bacon.

Serving suggestion
Serve with a selection of steamed vegetables or with salad.

Serves 4 to 8

Griot

Haiti

Ingredients
1.3 kg/3 lb leg of pork
2 large onions, finely chopped
3 hot green peppers, de-seeded and finely chopped
3 cloves garlic, crushed
150 ml/5 fl oz fresh unsweetened orange juice
Juice of 2 freshly squeezed limes
Salt and freshly ground pepper
Cooking oil
Water

Method
First create the marinade by mixing together the fruit juices, garlic, onions and peppers in a bowl. Season pork with salt and pepper and then add to marinade and leave overnight (minimum 8 to 10 hours). After marinating, place all the ingredients of the marinade and pork in a Dutch oven. Cover with water and bring to the boil, then lower the heat, cover and simmer for 1 hour, or until the liquid has evaporated. Heat cooking oil and fry the drained pork until it is brown all over.

Serving suggestion
Serve hot with rice and watercress salad.

Serves 5 to 6

Ham Roll

Dominica

Ingredients
450 g/1 lb rump steak
110 g/4 oz bacon
1 medium onion, finely chopped
2 eggs, size 2, beaten
2 tablespoons tomato paste
1 clove garlic, crushed
2 sprigs fresh thyme, leaves removed
Dash of Worcestershire sauce

Method
Mince or process bacon and steak, then combine with seasoning. Add Worcestershire sauce, tomato and eggs to meats and mix well. Grease an enamel bowl and place mixture inside, shaping into a roll. Steam for 1 hour then turn out onto a serving dish and sprinkle with toasted breadcrumbs.

Serving suggestion
Serve with boiled rice and fried plantain or green bananas and baked tomatoes.

Serves 6

Jerk Pork

Jamaica

Ingredients
1.3 kg/3 lbs pork shoulder, thickly sliced
4 scotch bonnet peppers, de-seeded
3 spring onions
3 cloves garlic
3 bay leaves, crushed
3 pimento (allspice), ground
2 teaspoons brown sugar

Method
Blend all the ingredients, except the pork, to create a smooth paste seasoning. Cut slits into the pork and generously rub in the seasoning, ensuring that all the meat is covered, and leave to marinate for 8 to 12 hours. Afterwards, place the meat in a steamer and cook for half an hour. Transfer the steamed pork to a roasting tin and cook in the oven at gas mark 4, 350°F, 180°C, for 1½ hours or until the pork is well cooked.

Serving suggestion
Serve with rice or with a tomato salad, or as a snack on its own.

Serves 4

Author's note: The cooked pork will be blackened. Do not worry, this is how it should look. Jerk pork is a very old recipe that was, until fairly recently, restricted to the Portland region of Jamaica. Nowadays, the jerk seasoning recipe is also used for chicken and fish.

Jug-Jug

Barbados

Ingredients

110 g/4 oz pickled pig's tail
230 g/8 oz salted beef
2 skinned chicken legs
2 medium onions, finely
chopped
1 stalk celery, finely chopped
425 ml/15 fl oz coconut milk
450 g/1 lb pigeon/gungo peas

60 g/2 oz finely ground
cornmeal
4 cloves garlic, crushed
2 sprigs thyme, chopped
1 sprig parsley, finely
chopped
60 g/2 oz unsalted butter
3 tablespoons cooking oil

Method

Place all the meats into a large pot or soup kettle and cover with cold water, replace lid and bring to the boil, then simmer until the beef is tender and easily shredded, about 1° to 2 hours. Allow to cool and then shred all the meat. Meanwhile, boil peas in another pot until tender, about 1 hour. If canned peas are used, these should just be heated through. Mince or finely chop the parsley, thyme, garlic, onion, peppers and celery. Make the cornmeal in a pan, according to instructions, then make into a paste with the coconut milk using 1 oz butter added to the cornmeal and then cooked with remainder of milk for 20 minutes, stirring frequently, over a low heat. Melt the remainder of the butter with some oil in a frying pan and add the seasonings and fry over a low heat until soft. Then add the shredded meats and black pepper and mix well. Mash the cooked peas and add to the cornmeal, and then add to the seasoning and meats. Mix well and then place in a greased pudding basin and leave to stand for a while. Turn out, cut into wedges and serve.

Serves 4

Oil Down

Grenada

Ingredients
900 g/2 lbs pigs' tails
900 ml/1½ pints coconut milk
1 large breadfruit, peeled, cored and cubed
1 large onion, finely chopped
1 hot green pepper
2 cloves garlic, chopped
3 sprigs thyme, finely chopped
3 sprigs parsley, finely chopped
3 teaspoons turmeric

Method
Soak the pigs' tails in cold water for 1 hour, then drain and rinse. Place in a large pot with the breadfruit and coconut milk, bring to the boil, then cover and simmer for 15 minutes. Add hot pepper and remaining ingredients, then simmer until meat is tender, about 40 minutes. Remove pepper before serving.

Serving suggestion
Serve hot on its own or with rice.

Serves 5 to 6

Pepperpot

Antigua

Ingredients
230 g/8 oz pigs' trotters
230 g/8 oz salt beef, diced
230 g/8 oz goat meat (shoulder or leg), diced
450 g/1 lb callaloo, chopped
450 g/1 lb cooked green peas
4 medium eggplants, diced
4 okra, topped and tailed, diced
2 medium onions, roughly chopped
2 medium tomatoes, chopped
4 tablespoons peeled and diced pumpkin
1 bunch spring onion
3 sprigs thyme
Salt and freshly ground black pepper

Method
Soak salt beef in water for 1 hour then place in a large pot and cover with cold water. Add the rest of the meats and bring to the boil, skim, and then simmer until nearly cooked, about 3 hours. Add all the vegetables, except the peas and spring onion, and cook for a further 25 minutes until mixture is thick. Add spring onions, thyme and green peas and cook for another 5 minutes and serve.

Serves 4

Pepperpot

Guyana

Ingredients
900 g/2 lb lean pork
1 boiling chicken
1 chopped oxtail
2 medium onions, finely chopped
4 hot red peppers, de-seeded
150 ml/5 fl oz cassareep (see page 291)
1 bunch thyme
3 tablespoons brown sugar
Water

Method
Joint the chicken and cut the meat into cubes. Place in a large pot of cold water with the chopped oxtail and simmer covered for 2 hours. Then add the remainder of the ingredients and simmer again until the meat is quite tender and the sauce is thick. Serve hot.

Serves 6 to 8

Pork Stew

St Lucia

Ingredients
1.8 kg/4 lb pork shoulder, cubed
450 g/1 lb onions, chopped
450 g/1 lb cucumbers, diced
230 g/8 oz carrots
230 g/8 oz tomatoes, skinned and chopped
110 g/4 oz green cabbage, shredded
1 leek, white part only
1 stick celery, finely chopped
4 cloves garlic, chopped
3 cloves, crushed
2 sprigs parsley, chopped
1 sprig thyme
230 g/8 oz unsalted butter
30 g/1 oz cooking oil
Salt and peppers to taste

Method
Heat cooking oil and butter in a large stew pot, add the leek, thyme, celery and onion and sauté until tender. Then, add pork, garlic, tomato, cabbage, carrots and salt and pepper and simmer for about 1½ hours until pork is tender. Then add cucumbers and cloves and simmer for a further 15 to 20 minutes. If required, thicken sauce with 2 teaspoons of arrowroot and two teaspoons of cold water. When cooked, sprinkle with chopped parsley before serving.

Serving suggestion
Serve with rice or yam, boiled or creamed potatoes.

Serves 8 to 10

Pow

Trinidad and Tobago

Ingredients
230 g/8 oz cooked roast pork, chopped
60 g/2 oz cornflour
1 teaspoon salt
1 teaspoon sugar
2 teaspoons dark soy sauce
120 ml/4 fl oz cooking oil
120 ml/4 fl oz water

Dough (for dumplings)
340 g/12 oz plain flour
110 g/4 oz sugar
120 ml/4 fl oz groundnut oil
60 ml/2 fl oz boiling water
1 teaspoon baking powder
½ teaspoon salt

Method
Start by preparing the dough. Add the sugar to boiling water, stir until dissolved, then set aside and allow to cool. Sift the flour, baking powder and salt into a large bowl, then make a well in the flour and slowly pour in the groundnut oil, then add the cold water. Combine the ingredients until a smooth dough is formed (if mixture is too wet, add small amounts of flour). Break off pieces of dough and flatten each piece into 8 cm/3 inch rounds. Mix cornflour with water. Heat the cooking oil in a large frying pan and add the chopped pork. Stir over a high heat for two minutes, add the soy sauce and seasonings, then add the cornflour mixture. Stir all the ingredients together and cook for a few minutes on a moderate heat until the sauce thickens. Allow to cool.

To assemble the dumplings, place a teaspoon of the pork filling in the centre of the dumpling rounds then draw the sides towards the centre and seal with cold water. Then place the dumplings in a steamer and cook for 20 minutes.

Serving suggestion
This Chinese dish may be eaten on its own as a snack with hot or soy sauce, or as part of a main meal.

Makes 12

Author's note: Traditionally, this dish was made with pork fat, but this recipe is a healthier option. For those who do not eat pork, other types of meat, fish or pak choi make ideal substitutes.

Steamed Wild Boar

Jamaica

Ingredients

900 g/2 lbs wild boar (see Author's note)
2 medium onions, chopped
½ large green capsicum, de-seeded
1 clove garlic, crushed
12 coriander seeds, crushed
2 tablespoons tomato puree
2 teaspoons finely grated orange rind
Juice of one orange
60 g/2 oz unsalted butter
Cooking oil
Salted water
Salt and freshly ground black pepper

Method

Remove the meat from the bones and cut into 5 cm/2-inch cubes. Place meat and bones in a pot of salt water, bring to the boil, then simmer for 1 to 2 hours or until meat is tender. Drain and reserve a quarter of the water. Sauté the meat in cooking oil until brown. Then sauté the onion, capsicum and garlic in butter until onion is tender. Stir in the tomato, orange rind and juice, coriander seeds, reserved water and salt and pepper. Cook until sauce has thickened and reduced. Add meat and cook for another 10 minutes on a low heat. Serve hot

Serving suggestion

Serve with creamed potatoes or creamed yam and steamed cabbage.

Serves 4 to 6

Author's note: Wild boar is available in specialist butchers and some supermarkets during the game season in Britain and the United States. If it is not available, use organic pork, which has more flavour than the non-organic variety.

Suckling Pig

Dominica

Ingredients
4.5-5.4 kg/10-12 lb oven-ready suckling pig
1 orange
4 cloves garlic
Vinegar
Sea salt

Stuffing
110 g/4 oz smoked bacon
2 large onions, chopped
1 hot red pepper
2 tablespoons tomato paste
2 bundles chives
1 bundle parsley
2 sprigs thyme
2 teaspoons season-all
2 cloves garlic
Dash of Worcestershire sauce
Dash of Angostura Bitters
Pigs' blood, if available
150 ml/5 fl oz olive oil
Salt and freshly ground black pepper

Method
Cut up the bacon, chives, thyme, parsley, onion and hot pepper and fry gently in hot oil. Allow to cool, then stir in the pigs' blood, stirring constantly to prevent curdling. Add the remainder of the ingredients to the cool mixture. Wipe the inside and outside of the suckling pig with vinegar, salt and garlic, then stuff it with the mixture. Either sew up the cavity or close with skewers. Place an onion in the pig's mouth and

smear butter over the skin. Bake in a moderate oven for 4 to 6 hours, basting frequently. If the pig is browning too quickly, cover with tin foil. When cooked, remove and serve on a large platter. Decorate with salad greens and fruit. Replace the onion with an orange in the mouth.

Serving suggestion
Roast suckling pig is usually prepared for Christmas or very festive occasions. This recipe is ideal for large supper parties and may be served with a selection of seasonal roast and steamed vegetables. The meat is usually sweet and tender.

Serves 10 to 12

Fish

Ackee and Saltfish

Jamaica

Ingredients
900 g/2 lb saltfish
230 g/8 oz ripe tomatoes, skinned and chopped
2 medium onions, finely chopped
1 green scotch bonnet pepper, de-seeded and finely chopped
2 tins ackee, drained
150 ml/5 fl oz malt vinegar
Freshly ground black pepper
Cooking oil

Method
Start by soaking the saltfish overnight (see Author's note). Next day, change the water and bring to the boil. Discard the water 3 times to remove the salt and then boil again for 15 minutes on a moderate heat or until fish flakes easily. Meanwhile, sauté the onions, pepper and tomatoes in 3 tablespoons of cooking oil, and when onion is tender, add the skinned, boned and flaked fish. Pour over vinegar, bring to the boil and simmer for 1 minute. Add the drained ackees and combine carefully so that they do not disintegrate too much, then add black pepper and serve hot.

Serving suggestion
Serve for breakfast or a light lunch with Johnny cakes and fried plantain.

Serves 4 to 6

Author's note: Some people skin and bone the saltfish before cooking, and others do it after cooking, when the fish flakes easily.

Blaff

Martinique

Ingredients
900 g/2 lb red snapper or kingfish, whole
2 whole red peppers, de-seeded and finely chopped
5 spring onions, chopped
½ yellow capsicum, de-seeded and cut into thin rings
3 cloves garlic, crushed
6 sprigs parsley
3 sprigs thyme
¾ teaspoon ground allspice
Juice of 2 freshly squeezed limes

Method
Clean and scale the fish, then place in a large dish and marinate for 2-3 hours in lime juice, 1 crushed clove garlic, capsicum and ½ teaspoon of allspice. Fill a large saucepan with cold water, add half the parsley, garlic, spring onions and remainder of the allspice. Bring to the boil, then add the fish, including the marinade, and cook for 20 minutes on a low heat. Lift out fish and discard seasonings. Garnish with hot pepper and the remaining parsley.

Serving suggestion
Serve with rice or potatoes and a salad.

Serves 4 to 5

Breaded King Fish

Bahamas

Ingredients
900 g/2 lb king fish, cleaned and sliced
2 eggs, size 3, lightly stirred
170 g/6 oz fresh white breadcrumbs
2 limes
3 teaspoons paprika
Salt and freshly ground black pepper
Cooking oil

Method
Wash and dry the fish, then season with salt and pepper. Mix paprika with the breadcrumbs. Dip the fish slices into the stirred egg then into the breadcrumbs. Heat the oil in a large frying pan, then add the slices and cook over a high heat until the fish is golden brown on both sides, about 3 minutes per side.

Serving suggestion
Serve hot, garnished with lime wedges and serve with French fries and a mixed salad.

Serves 4

Brown Fish Stew

Jamaica

Ingredients
900 g/2 lb kingfish or red snapper fillets
2 medium onions, sliced
2 chopped tomatoes
4 slices red scotch bonnet pepper
1 clove garlic, chopped
1 tablespoon pimento berries
Juice of two limes
360 ml/12 fl oz water
Freshly ground black pepper
Cooking oil
Salt

Method
Clean and wash the fish, then rub with lime juice. Pat dry with kitchen towel. Heat cooking oil in a frying pan until smoking hot. Add fish fillets and fry on both sides until crisp and brown. Drain out oil from pan, leaving enough to coat the bottom, then add tomatoes, pimento, garlic, scotch bonnet pepper slices, onion and black pepper, and fry until onion is soft, then add water and salt. Bring to the boil and reduce by half, then cover and simmer for 10 minutes.

Serving suggestion
Serve hot with rice or turned cornmeal and steamed buttered carrots or cabbage.

Serves 4

Brule Johl

Trinidad

Ingredients
450 g/1 lb saltfish, soaked overnight
2 small red capsicums, de-seeded and diced
2 small green capsicums, de-seeded and diced
1 bunch spring onions, finely chopped
3 tablespoons extra virgin olive oil
2 teaspoons hot pepper sauce
1 tablespoon fresh lime juice

Method
Skin and bone the saltfish, then flake into a bowl. Mix olive oil, lime juice, hot pepper sauce, spring onions and red and green peppers together, and combine with fish. Refrigerate for 2 hours before serving, stirring occasionally.

Serving suggestion
Serve as stuffing for avocado pears or as a light snack on toast.

Serves 4 to 5

Classic Caribbean Cooking

Cascadura Curry

Trinidad

Ingredients
12 cascuduras, cleaned and scaled
1.2 litres/2 pints coconut milk
150 ml/5 fl oz fish stock, made from fish heads
2 medium onions, finely chopped
1 hot red pepper, de-seeded and finely chopped
4 cloves garlic, crushed
4 sprigs thyme, finely chopped
2 sprigs coriander, finely chopped
4 tablespoons curry powder
½ teaspoon caraway seeds
Juice of 2 freshly squeezed limes
Salt and freshly ground black pepper
Cooking oil
Water

Method
Make a paste with water, curry powder, and 1 clove of garlic, onion and caraway seeds. Wash the fish with lime juice and leave for 10 minutes. Dry fish on kitchen paper, then spread with coriander, remaining garlic, thyme and pepper. Heat oil in a frying pan and add paste, then cook for 2 minutes. Add the fish and cook for a further 2 minutes. Add fish stock and coconut milk and cook covered for 20 minutes.

Serving suggestion
Serve hot with rice or roti and chutney.

Serves 6

Creole Fish Stew

Guyana

Ingredients
4 fillets red snapper
110 g/4 oz coconut cream
230 g/8 oz tomatoes, skinned and chopped
2 large onions, finely chopped
3 cloves garlic, crushed
1 tablespoon Worcestershire sauce
2 teaspoons garlic powder
1 teaspoon English mustard powder
1 sprig thyme
Salt and freshly ground black pepper

Method
Wash the fish well, then dry on kitchen paper and season with salt, pepper, Worcester sauce, garlic powder and mustard. Rub well into the fish and leave to marinate overnight. Fry fillets in deep hot oil and drain. Make the sauce by placing the tomatoes into a saucepan with the thyme and coconut cream. Bring to the boil, then simmer for 10 minutes. Sauté the onions and garlic in the cooking oil, then add to the sauce. Finally, add the fried fish and let the whole dish simmer for 3-4 minutes before serving.

Serving suggestion
Serve with rice or potatoes and a selection of fresh vegetables.

Serves 3 to 4

Escovitch Fish

Jamaica

Ingredients
1.3 kg/3 lb goat fish or small red snapper
3 large onions, sliced
2 limes, cut and squeezed
1 green scotch bonnet pepper, de-seeded and cut into fine strips
1½ teaspoons pimento berries
450 ml/15 fl oz malt vinegar
150 ml/5 fl oz oil for frying
4 teaspoons freshly ground black pepper
4 teaspoons salt

Method
In a large saucepan combine vinegar, onions, pimento berries and three whole black peppercorns and simmer until onions are tender then remove from the heat and allow to cool. Wash fish in water and lime juice, then dry well with kitchen paper and season with salt and pepper. Heat oil to smoking point in a heavy frying pan, and then fry the fish swiftly on both sides until crisp. Place fish in a deep dish or bowl and pour over the cooled onions and vinegar. Leave overnight in the refrigerator before serving.

Serving suggestion
Ideal with fried potatoes, plain boiled rice or fried plantain, and a green salad as a main course.

Serve 4 to 6

Fish and Macaroni Pie

Bermuda

Ingredients
900 g/2 lb white fish
340 g/12 oz 'quick cook' thin macaroni
2 eggs, hard boiled, chopped
4 black pepper corns
1 bayleaf
½ carrot, peeled
Salt and ground black pepper

Sauce
300 ml/10 fl oz milk
60 g/2 oz butter
60 g/2 oz cornflour
3 teaspoons English mustard powder
Fresh breadcrumbs

Method
Simmer fish in a little milk with half a carrot, bay leaf and black peppercorns. Drain and reserve liquid for the sauce. In a pan of salted water boil the macaroni for the required cooking time. Drain then add to a buttered oven-proof dish, alternating with layers of fish and macaroni with the chopped eggs in the middle. Make the sauce by melting the butter and then adding the mustard and cornflour. Mix to a smooth paste and gradually add the cold milk while stirring constantly. Finish off by mixing in the reserved strained milk. Mix until sauce is thick, then pour over the fish and macaroni, sprinkle with fresh breadcrumbs and bake in a moderate oven at gas mark 4, 350°F, 180°C, until the pie is hot and the top is browned.

Serving suggestion
Serve hot with a green vegetable or sautéed carrots.

Serves 4 to 6

Classic Caribbean Cooking

Fried Flying Fish

Barbados

Ingredients
4 flying fish, boned
2 tablespoons plain flour
2 large eggs
2 limes
1 teaspoon salt

Freshly ground black
pepper
Oil for frying
Water

Method
Fillet the fish by cutting it from the head along the stomach to the tail, remove the viscera (innards), and rinse the cavity under cold running water. Lay the fish cut-side down on some kitchen paper and with a firm hand, press along the backbone and the majority of the bones should come away cleanly. If some bones are left, remove them with sterile tweezers. Wash the fish thoroughly in cold water and lime juice, then drain and pat dry with kitchen paper. Make the batter by placing flour, salt and pepper in a bowl and adding enough cold water until a smooth paste is formed, then thin with water until the mixture is the consistency of thick custard. Heat the oil in a deep fat fryer, wok or large frying pan, coat the fish in batter, and fry. Depending on the size of the fish, cooking time should take between eight and ten minutes. Serve hot with slices of lime.

Serving suggestion
This can be served with salad or vegetables, including fried potatoes, plantain or yam chips.

Serves 4

Author's note: If you are unable to obtain flying fish, herring is a good substitute.

Keshy Yena coe Pisca

Curaçao

Ingredients

450 g/1 lb red snapper, filleted
1.8 kg/4 lb Edam cheese
2 large tomatoes, skinned and chopped
1 large onion, finely chopped
12 green olives (stuffed with pimento)
2 tablespoons finely chopped sweet pickled cucumbers
80 g/3 oz seedless raisins
2 eggs, size 2, well beaten
170 g/6 oz fresh breadcrumbs, fine
1 teaspoon cayenne pepper
Salt and ground black pepper

Method

Peel off red wax coating from the cheese and cut an inch thick slice from the top (lid), then set aside. Scoop out the cheese from the centre, making sure you leave about 1 cm/½ inch casing. Grate the extracted cheese and reserve 110 g/4 oz. Fill the hollowed-out cheese with cold water and soak the lid in cold water for an hour. Place the fish fillets in a pan, cover with cold water and simmer for 7 minutes or until the fish flakes easily when tested with a fork. Heat butter in a frying pan and sauté the onion. Add the tomatoes, cayenne pepper, salt and pepper, stirring constantly until the mixture is thick. Add the breadcrumbs, olives, pickled cucumbers, raisins and grated cheese, combine well, then add the fish. Fold in the eggs, then stuff the mixture into the drained and dried cheese case. Place the stuffed cheese into a buttered deep casserole, replace the cheese lid, cover and bake at gas mark 4, 350°F, 180°C, for 30 minutes. When cooked, cut into wedges and serve.

Serves 8

Classic Caribbean Cooking

Lapped Herring

Barbados

Ingredients
450 g/1 lb herring, cleaned, filleted and skinned
2 eggs, size 2
Freshly ground black pepper

Method
Whisk eggs until frothy then add freshly ground black pepper.
Dip herrings into egg mixture and fry until golden brown.

Serving suggestion
Serve with bread or with scrambled eggs.

Serves 4

Pickled Red Herring

Virgin Islands

Ingredients
4 large red herring
2 large onions, finely chopped
1 hot green pepper
300 ml/10 fl oz white wine vinegar

Method
Place vinegar, onions and pepper in a large bowl, mix together and transfer to a large preserving jar. Skin and fillet the herrings, then chop into small pieces and place in the jar. Stir, then leave overnight.

Serving suggestion
Serve cold with crackers, or for a more substantial meal with a mixed salad.

Serves 6

Poached Red Snapper with Herbed Avocado Sauce

Jamaica

Ingredients

2 medium red snapper
2 large avocados, pureed
with 4 teaspoons lime
½ an avocado, sliced
1 medium onion, chopped
300 ml/10 fl oz dry white wine

3 sprigs thyme
3 sprigs coriander
2 teaspoons lime juice
1 lime
150 ml/5 fl oz water

Method

Wash and scale fish, then fillet. Poach in a liquid of water and wine, with a sprig of coriander, onions, two slices of lime and two sprigs of thyme. Poach fish on a very low heat for 5-6 minutes. Meanwhile, puree the avocado with lime juice, thyme and coriander in a blender or processor. Lift out fish with a slotted spoon. Serve hot on a warm plate with sauce poured over the fish, and garnish with the avocado slices

Serving suggestion

Serve with sautéed potatoes or yam chips and sautéed mushrooms.

Serves 2

Author's note: Avocado flesh turns brown (oxidises) once peeled. To avoid this, add lime or lemon juice to the flesh when peeled.

Run Down

Jamaica

Ingredients
450 g/1 lb mackerel fillets
750 ml/1¼ pints coconut milk
450 g/1 lb tomatoes, skinned and chopped
1 large onion, finely chopped
2 cloves garlic, finely chopped
3 tablespoons lime juice
1 tablespoon malt vinegar
1 tablespoon de-seeded, finely chopped green scotch bonnet pepper (Scotch bonnet peppers are very hot, for a milder flavour reduce the amount)
1 sprig thyme
Salt and freshly ground black pepper

Method
Marinate the cleaned fish in lime juice for half an hour turning once. Cook the coconut milk in a heavy frying pan until the coconut milk is oily. Next, add onion and garlic and cook until onion is tender. Add the scotch bonnet pepper, salt, black pepper, malt vinegar, thyme and tomatoes, and stir and cook gently for 10 minutes. Drain the fish, then add to the frying pan with the other ingredients, cook on a low heat until fish is tender, about 10 minutes.

Serving suggestion
Serve hot with boiled green bananas.

Serves 4

Classic Caribbean Cooking

Salt Cod, Scrambled Eggs and Crab

Dominican Republic

Ingredients
450 g/1 lb salt cod, skinned, soaked and boned
900 g/2 lb crab meat with cartilage removed
150 ml/5 fl oz single cream
6 eggs, size 2, lightly beaten
4 cloves garlic, finely chopped
2 tablespoons parsley
3 tablespoons extra virgin olive oil
60 g/2 oz unsalted butter
Freshly ground black pepper

Method
Place the cod in cold water and bring to the boil. Discard water several times until saltiness has been removed, then cook for 20 minutes. Allow to cool, then flake. Heat the butter with a tablespoon of oil in a large frying pan, add the crab meat, flaked cod and garlic and cook for 5 minutes, stirring lightly from time to time. Add chopped parsley, fold in the eggs and cream, and scramble until lightly set. Season with black pepper.

Serving suggestion
Serve immediately for breakfast, brunch or a light meal, with Johnny cakes or hot buttered toast.

Serves 6

Saltfish and Paw-Paw

Jamaica

Ingredients
230 g/8 oz salt cod
900 g/2 lb green paw-paw (papaya)
6 rashers streaky bacon, chopped
2 medium onions, chopped
2 medium tomatoes, chopped and skinned
1 red scotch bonnet pepper, de-seeded
1 sprig fresh thyme
240 ml/8 fl oz water
Cooking oil

Method
Soak the cod in water overnight then boil in water for 15 minutes. Slice the paw-paw and discard the seeds. Heat the oil in a large frying pan, add chopped bacon and fry. Remove from the pan and set aside. Skin, bone and flake the fish. Add the onions, chopped thyme, tomatoes and pepper to the frying pan and cook until softened. Add the paw-paw and fish and cook in a covered pan until the paw-paw is tender and the liquid has reduced by half. Finally, add the bacon and cook for a further minute then serve.

Serving suggestion
Ideal with roasted breadfruit or boiled yam.

Serves 4

Serenata

Dominican Republic

Ingredients
450 g/1 lb salt cod
450 g/1 lb old potatoes
2 medium tomatoes, skinned and chopped
1 large avocado, skinned, stoned and chopped
4 stuffed green olives (stuffed with pimento), thinly sliced
1 bunch spring onions, finely chopped
120 ml/4 fl oz extra virgin olive oil
60 ml/2 fl oz white wine vinegar
Freshly ground black pepper

Method
Soak the salt cod in cold water overnight. The next day place in a saucepan with fresh cold water, bring to the boil and discard water twice. Refill and bring to the boil and simmer for 15 minutes or until cooked. Meanwhile, peel and cube the potatoes and boil in salted water. Drain when cooked, about 12 to 15 minutes. Flake the fish and remove all the bones and skin. Place with the potatoes in a salad bowl and add sliced avocado, olives, chopped tomatoes and spring onions. Pour over dressing made with olive oil and wine vinegar, and season with black pepper.

Serving suggestion
Serve with hot candied sweet potatoes and fried plantain.

Serves 5 to 6

Smoked Herring Choka

Guyana

Ingredients
4 smoked herrings
230 g/8 oz tomatoes, skinned and chopped
2 large onions, sliced
1 hot red pepper, de-seeded and chopped
5 cloves garlic, crushed
4 tablespoons corn oil
Freshly ground black pepper

Method
Remove heads and tails of the herrings, then place the fish in a fish kettle or large saucepan, cover with water, bring to the boil and cook for 10 minutes. Remove and drain, then apply pressure to the backbone of the fish and lift out as many bones as possible and remove others with sterile tweezers. Flake the fish. Add oil to a frying pan and add tomatoes, onions and garlic, then stir briskly while frying. This takes about 12 minutes for the onion and tomato to cook, then add the fish and combine.

Serving suggestion
Serve with corn oil drizzled over and with sada roti for breakfast or a light lunch.

Serves 4

Steamed Butter Fish

Jamaica

Ingredients
900 g/2 lb butter fish
1 medium onion
8 fresh slices ginger
1 tablespoon dry sherry
1 tablespoon light soy sauce
1 tablespoon vegetable oil
1 tablespoon water
½ teaspoon salt

Method
Clean the fish, dry well and score flesh on both sides in a diagonal pattern. Place on a fireproof plate or on a rack in a steamer. Sprinkle fish with sherry and salt, then pour over the oil, soy sauce and water. Shred ginger and onion and push into the cavities of the fish. Leave to stand for 10 minutes. Steam for 10 minutes. Serve garnished with fresh coriander.

Serving suggestion
Serve with creamed potatoes, okra in tomato sauce or rice and a selection of steamed vegetables.

Serves 4 as a main course

Steamed Fish

St Vincent

Ingredients
450 g/1 lb grouper
300 ml/10 fl oz white sauce (see page 282)
2 eggs, hard boiled, sliced
3 sprigs parsley
Vinegar
Freshly ground black pepper to taste
Salt
Water

Method
Wash fish in cold water and salt, then place on a rack in a fish kettle. Then pour in 900ml/1½ pints of water and add one dessert spoon of salt and two teaspoons of vinegar. Simmer gently for 20 minutes and drain thoroughly. Garnish with white sauce, parsley and sliced eggs.

Serving suggestion
Serve with a green vegetable and creamed potatoes.

Steamed Flying Fish

Barbados

Ingredients
4 flying fish
2 large onions, sliced
2 large tomatoes, sliced
2 sprigs fresh thyme
2 slices hot red pepper
1 tablespoon salted butter
1 tablespoon lime or lemon juice
Freshly ground black pepper
Salt

Method
Clean and bone flying fish (see page 77) then wash in water with lemon or lime juice. Pat dry with kitchen paper, then season well with salt and pepper. Carefully place tail into the mouth of fish (see Author's note), place in a dish and cover with slices of onion, tomatoes, thyme and hot pepper. Sprinkle lime juice over top and add two tablespoons of water. Finally, add butter and cook in a steamer for about 15 minutes or until fish is tender. Serve hot.

Serving suggestion
Serve with steamed vegetables such as cabbage, or callaloo and rice.

Serves 4

Author's note: To place the tail in the mouth of the fish adds nothing to the cooking procedure or taste, but is favoured by chefs for presentation. The fish should form a semi-circle once the tail is inserted into the mouth. You can, of course, leave out this part if you are in a hurry.

Tuna Sanoche

Dominica

Ingredients
450 g/1 lb fresh tuna
1 tin coconut milk
1 medium onion, chopped
4 blades chives, chopped
2 cloves garlic, crushed
1 teaspoon saffron (see Author's note)
1 teaspoon arrowroot
2 tablespoons butter
Cooking oil for frying
Salt and ground black pepper

Method
Clean and cut the fish into 6 portions, season with salt and pepper and fry for 3 minutes on each side in hot oil. In a large pot melt the butter with a tablespoon of oil and sauté the onions, garlic and chopped chives for 5 minutes. Add coconut milk and saffron, bring to the boil, reduce heat then add arrowroot mixed with water and stir until sauce has thickened. Finally, add the tuna and simmer for 5 minutes. Serve hot.

Serving suggestion
Serve with rice and green vegetables.

Serves 6

Author's note: Saffron should be steeped in one tablespoon of boiling water for 2 minutes before adding it, and the water, to the recipe.

Shellfish

Baked Crayfish in Banana Leaves

Jamaica

Ingredients
3 medium crayfish, live
360 ml/12 fl oz pimento liqueur (or any aniseed liqueur)
3 large banana leaves or tin foil (see Author's note)
170 g/6 oz unsalted butter

Method
First kill the crayfish. The simplest way is to put them head-first into a bucket or large bowl of ice water and leave for 1½ hours. Then spread softened butter over the banana leaves, lay one crayfish on each leaf and pour pimento liqueur over the crayfish. Wrap the leaf around each crayfish and tie securely with kitchen string. Bake in a shallow dish at gas mark 4, 350°F, 180°C, for 1 hour. Untie string, split crayfish with a cleaver or large knife and serve hot.

Serving suggestion
Serve with potato salad, green salad, plain boiled rice or rice and peas and fried plantain.

Serves 4 to 6

Author's note: Banana leaves are often available in Caribbean, Chinese or south Asian food shops.

Crabs in Pepper Sauce

Dominican Republic

Ingredients
450 g/1 lb crab meat
4 hot green peppers, de-seeded and chopped
4 medium tomatoes, skinned, de-seeded and chopped
1 large onion, finely chopped
1 green sweet pepper, de-seeded and chopped
4 cloves garlic, chopped
3 tablespoons tomato puree
2 tablespoons chopped parsley
150 ml/5 fl oz dry sherry
60 ml/2 fl oz olive oil
1 tablespoon lime juice
¼ teaspoon sugar
Freshly ground black pepper

Method
Remove any cartilage from the crab meat. Heat the oil in a heavy base frying pan and sauté the onions, garlic and peppers until the onions are tender. Add the tomato puree, tomatoes, salt, sugar and pepper and cook until the mixture is thick, about 10 minutes. Stir in the lime juice and sherry, add crab meat, stir then cover and cook on a low heat for 4 minutes. Garnish with parsley.

Serving suggestion
Serve with boiled white rice

Serves 4 to 6

Crayfish Creole

Dominica

Ingredients
3 crayfish
1 hot red pepper, de-seeded, chopped
1 lime
1 clove garlic, crushed
1 tablespoon unsalted butter
1 teaspoon chopped parsley
Freshly ground black pepper
Salt

Method
Wash the crayfish thoroughly with squeezed lime juice, then place in a large pot of boiling water for 20 minutes. Meanwhile, mix together the butter, garlic, parsley and red pepper to make a paste. Halve each crayfish lengthways and spread with the paste. Place in a greased dish and cook under a hot grill for 5 minutes and serve.

Serving suggestion
Serve on its own as a light lunch or as part of a main course

Serves 2 to 3

Author's note: Outside of the Caribbean, crayfish are sometimes difficult to find. However, it is worth the effort to seek them out as they are a delicious alternative to crab or lobster.

Curried Lambi

Dominica

Ingredients
900 g/2 lb lambi (conch)
1 medium onion, sliced
1 stalk celery
1 sprig thyme
1 clove garlic, crushed
60 g/2 oz curry powder (see page 292)
1 teaspoon dry English mustard
2 tablespoons butter
60 ml/2 fl oz oil

Method
Wash conch in water to remove any slime, then dry and pound with a steak mallet to break down fibres. Boil in salted water for about 1½ hours or until conch is tender. Remove conch from the water, allow to cool then dice. Heat oil in a large frying pan, add crushed garlic, onion, celery, mustard powder and curry powder, and stir until the onion is soft and the powders form a paste. Add diced conch (with a little of the water in which it was boiled), thyme, salt and pepper to taste, and continue cooking for a further 20 minutes. Stir in the butter just before serving.

Serving suggestion
Serve with rice and mango chutney.

Serves 6

Hot Gingered Prawns

Jamaica

Ingredients
680 g/1½ lbs unshelled prawns
1 tablespoon finely chopped onion
1 tablespoon rice wine or dry sherry
3 teaspoons dark soy sauce
2 teaspoons chicken stock powder or ½ chicken stock cube
3 teaspoons freshly grated ginger

Method
Shell the prawns, but leave tails on. Remove black vein by cutting into the back of the prawn, and wash under cold running water then pat dry on kitchen paper. Heat oil in a wok or large frying pan and sauté the ginger and onion briskly for ½ minute. Add wine, chicken stock powder and soy sauce, bring to the boil and simmer for 2 minutes. Add prawns and stir in sauce until prawns turn pink, about 2 minutes.

Serving suggestion
This Chinese-Jamaican dish goes very well with boiled rice or boiled or fried noodles.

Serves 4 to 6

Lambi Souse

Grenada

Ingredients
900 g/2 lb lambi (conch)
1½ medium onions, finely chopped
1 cucumber, chopped
1 sweet red pepper, de-seeded, for garnish
1 hot green pepper
300 ml/10 fl oz freshly squeezed lime juice
Salt

Method
Beat the conch with a steak hammer to tenderise. Place in a pressure cooker, covered with salt water and cook at high pressure for 30 minutes, or longer if the meat is still not tender. Cool in the liquid, then drain. Cut meat into bite-size pieces and place in a large glass preserving jar with onion, hot pepper, cucumber, lime juice and salt. Cover and refrigerate overnight.

Serving suggestion
Serve with boiled breadfruit.

Serves 4

Lobster Newburg

Antigua

Ingredients
1.8 kg/4 lb cooked lobster
300 ml/10 fl oz whipping cream
4 egg yolks, size 2
2 tablespoons rum
2 tablespoons sherry
110 g/4 oz unsalted butter
Pinch cayenne pepper
Pinch grated nutmeg
Toast

Method
Pick out the lobster meat from within the shell, then fry in butter over a low heat. Add nutmeg and pepper and salt if required. Beat the egg yolks together with the cream, then stir into the cooked meat. Add rum and sherry and continue to stir with a wooden spoon until the mixture thickens. Serve at once on hot, buttered slices of toast.

Serving suggestion
Serve as a fish course, a starter, or as a light lunch with a green salad.

Serves 6 to 8

Lobster Rissoles

St Kitts

Ingredients
1 large lobster, boiled and picked over to remove cartilage
150 ml/5 fl oz milk
3 eggs
2 hard boiled egg yolks
3 tablespoons plain flour
4 drops hot pepper sauce
Salt and freshly ground black pepper
Cooking oil for frying

Method
Finely mince or chop lobster meat and mix with egg yolks, pepper sauce, salt and pepper. Sift the flour and beat in the eggs, then add enough milk to form a smooth stiff batter, then add the lobster. If the mixture is too wet, add more flour, one tablespoon at a time. Mixture should be thick enough to be rolled into medium-sized fingers, then fry until golden brown on all sides in moderately hot cooking oil. Drain and serve.

Serving suggestion
Serve hot or cold with a green salad or as a snack with drinks.

Serves 2 to 6

Okra Stew with Shrimps

Barbados

Ingredients
450 g/1 lb shelled prawns or shrimps
230 g/8 oz okras, topped, tailed, sliced
230 g/8 oz cooked sweet corn
3 medium tomatoes, skinned and chopped
2 medium sweet capsicums, de-seeded and diced
1 green hot pepper, whole
6 tablespoons chopped spring onion
1 fresh bay leaf
1 tablespoon tomato paste
1 tablespoon freshly squeezed lime juice
4 tablespoons butter
Salt and freshly ground black pepper to taste

Method
Mix the lime juice with the shellfish and set aside. Heat the butter in a frying pan and sauté the onions and green pepper for 3 minutes. Add all the remaining ingredients to the pan and simmer for 10 minutes. Add the shellfish and bring to the boil, then simmer for 5 minutes. Remove the whole pepper and bay leaf before serving.

Serving suggestion
Serve with plain boiled rice.

Serves 4 to 5

Peppered Crabs

Trinidad and Tobago

Ingredients
2 medium crabs, live
3 spring onions, chopped
1 red capsicum, chopped
1 green hot pepper, fresh, de-seeded
3 cloves garlic, chopped
6 fresh slices ginger
4 teaspoons chilli sauce
1 tablespoon soy sauce
1 tablespoon lime juice
1 teaspoon cayenne pepper
1 teaspoon sugar
60 ml/2 fl oz cold water

Method
Place live crabs into a large pan of boiling water and remove when the shells turns pink. Allow to cool. Remove stomach bag, hard shell top and fibrous tissue, wash and then chop each crab into 4 equal pieces. Blend capsicum, cayenne pepper, garlic and spring onions to create a smooth paste. Pour into a large frying pan or wok and stir-fry for 3 minutes. Add lime, soy sauce, chilli sauce, sugar, ginger and pepper and stir well. Add crab portions and leave for 1 minute, then pour in the water and cover and simmer for 15 minutes. Serve hot with sauce poured over the crab.

Serves 4

Prawns Creole

Jamaica

Ingredients
450 g/1 lb raw prawns, shelled
150 ml/5 fl oz coconut cream
110 g/4 oz cashew nuts
110 g/4 oz mushrooms, sliced
1 medium onion, sliced
1 stick celery, finely sliced
½ red capsicum, sliced and de-seeded
1 clove garlic, sliced
1 cm/½ inch fresh ginger
1 tablespoon cooking oil
1 teaspoon Worcestershire sauce
Pinch salt
Hot pepper sauce (according to taste)

Method
Heat oil in a heavy frying pan or wok. Add onions, pepper and garlic and sauté until onions are golden, taking care not to burn the garlic. Add mushrooms and celery and cook for a further two minutes. Remove garlic, add coconut cream, Worcestershire sauce, salt, hot pepper sauce, cashews and finely sliced ginger, and cook for a further three minutes. Add the prawns and cook on a gentle heat for 4 minutes.

Serving suggestion
Serve hot with boiled rice and steamed callaloo.

Serves 3 as a main course

Roast Lobster

St Lucia

Ingredients
1 large, cooked lobster
450 g/1 lb carrots, grated
1 large head lettuce
1 lemon, quartered
4 cloves garlic, finely chopped
2 sprigs parsley
450 g/1 lb unsalted butter

Method
Cook the garlic in butter for 5 minutes over a low heat. Cut the lobster in half, lengthways, and remove the meat, do not break the tail away from the head. Remove the intestines from the lobster meat and discard. Chop the meat in cubes. Wash lobster head well. Pile the lobster meat back into washed shell. Pour the melted garlic butter over the lobster, and then place lobster on a dish of shredded lettuce and grated carrot, garnished with lemon wedges.

Serving suggestion
Serve with potato, green or mixed salad.

Serves 2 as a starter, or 1 as a main course

Shrimp and Coconut

Barbados

Ingredients
450 g/1 lb uncooked shrimps
170 g/6 oz fresh coconut, grated
3 ripe tomatoes, sliced
2 medium onions, minced
1 hot green pepper, de-seeded
2 cloves garlic, minced
4 tablespoons freshly squeezed lime juice
Freshly ground white pepper

Method
Shell and wash shrimps and place in a dish with all but 4 teaspoons of lime juice. Marinate for ½ hour. Blend onions, pepper and garlic to form a puree, then combine with the drained shrimps. Add the remaining lime juice to the coconut, add salt and pepper and mix well into the shrimp mixture. Spread half the amount of tomatoes onto tin foil and spread the shrimp mixture over them. Spread the remaining tomatoes on top and cover and seal with tin foil to create a foil package. Bake in a pre-heated oven at gas mark 4, 350°F, 180°C, for 35 minutes, turning once during cooking time.

Serves 3 as a starter

Shrimp Curry

Guyana

Ingredients
450 g/1 lb shrimps
150 ml/5 fl oz coconut milk
1 onion, finely chopped
1 clove garlic, finely chopped
2 tablespoons curry powder
2 tablespoons tamarind juice
80 g/3 oz unsalted butter
Salt and freshly ground black pepper

Method
Heat butter in a large saucepan, add onion and garlic and cook over a low heat until softened. Stir in curry powder and cook for two minutes, then add the tamarind juice and coconut milk with salt and pepper to taste. Cook until slightly thickened, add the shrimps and cook over a low heat for a further 5 minutes or until tender. Shake the pan to prevent sticking.

Serving suggestion
Serve with plain boiled rice

Serves 4

Shrimps and Rice

Grenada

Ingredients
450 g/1 lb fresh shrimps
80 g/3 oz salt pork
280 g/10 oz white rice
2 large onions, chopped
2 tomatoes, skinned, chopped
½ green capsicum, chopped
1 stick celery
1 clove garlic, peeled
2 tablespoons tomato ketchup
1 tablespoon chopped parsley
1 teaspoon dark soy sauce
¼ teaspoon salt
360 ml/12 fl oz water

Method
Cut the pork into small pieces and fry with the garlic, chopped onions, capsicum, parsley, celery and tomatoes for five minutes on a medium heat, stirring occasionally to prevent sticking. Add the rice, water, salt and tomato ketchup, and bring to the boil. Reduce heat and cook covered for 10 minutes. Add the shrimps and soy sauce and cook for a further 10 minutes.

Serving suggestion
Serve with fried plantain or fried green bananas.

Serves 4 as a main course

Classic Caribbean Cookery

Vegetarian

Aunt Florrie's Creamed Potatoes

Jamaica

Ingredients
900 g/2 lbs old potatoes
150 g/5 fl oz milk
80 g/3 oz butter
1 tablespoon mayonnaise
Freshly ground black pepper
Salt

Method
Peel and cut the potatoes to the same size, lengthways, then put them in a large saucepan, add salt, and cover with cold water. Bring to the boil, cover and simmer for 20 minutes, or until cooked. Drain the water, then mash until smooth. Add mayonnaise, black pepper and butter and mix well, then add the milk, beat well, then serve hot.

Serving suggestion
Serve as an accompaniment to any main course as an alternative to rice or yam.

Serves 4 to 5

Avocado Salad

Haiti

Ingredients
1 large Caribbean avocado
110 g/4 oz green olives stuffed with pimento
1 large head of lettuce
150 g/5 fl oz French dressing

Method
Shred lettuce into a salad bowl. Peel and stone the avocado with a stainless steel knife. Slice thinly and add to the bowl. Drizzle French dressing over salad and garnish with sliced stuffed olives.

Serving suggestion
Serve as an accompaniment to rice and peas or on its own as a starter.

Serves 4 to 6

Baked Green Bananas

Jamaica

Ingredients
8 green bananas
150 ml/5 fl oz milk
60 g/2 oz butter
110 g/4 oz white breadcrumbs
2 tablespoons grated cheese
2 tablespoons finely chopped spring onion
1 sprig thyme
2 teaspoons salt

Method
Top and tail the bananas but do not peel, then cook them in salted water until tender, about 20 minutes. Then drain, peel and mash until the mixture is smooth. Add seasonings and milk then place in a buttered, oven-proof dish. Sprinkle cheese and breadcrumbs on top and bake at gas mark 4, 350°F, 180°C, for 25 minutes or until evenly browned.

Serving suggestion
Serve with rice and peas.

Serves 6 to 8

Baked Yam with Corn and Cheese

Jamaica

Ingredients
1.8 kg/4 lb yellow yam
1 corn on the cob
1 red capsicum, de-seeded and cut into rings
1 green capsicum, de-seeded and cut into rings
1 medium onion, chopped
230 g/8 oz unsalted butter
110 g/4 oz cheddar cheese
Pinch of paprika
Salt

Method
Peel and dice the yam, then boil in salted water until tender. Drain and mash with butter. While yam is still warm, cook corn in water, and when tender, drain and remove kernels from the cob and mix with the yam. Soften onion in butter with all but two rings of the red and green capsicum. Grease a shallow, oven-proof dish and spread the yam mixture evenly within. Grate the cheese and sprinkle over the mixture, top with reserved capsicum rings. Bake in a moderate oven, gas mark 5, 375°F, 190°C, for 15 minutes or until golden brown.

Serving suggestion
Serve as a light lunch with salad or rice and fried plantain.

Serves 2 as a lunch dish or 4 as a side dish

Boiled Cucumbers

St Lucia

Ingredients
12 cucumbers, peeled and sliced thickly lengthways
4 tablespoons unsalted butter or margarine
Salt and freshly ground black pepper

Method
Place the cucumbers in boiling salted water and cook for ten minutes. Remove and spread with melted butter and sprinkle with salt and pepper.

Serving suggestion
Serve with rice, potatoes and a selection of vegetables.

Serves 12 as a side dish or 3 as part of a main course

Boiled Pumpkin

Barbados

Ingredients
450 g/1 lb pumpkin, peeled, sliced and de-seeded
2 tablespoons unsalted butter
Salt and freshly ground black pepper
1.2 litres/2 pints water

Method
Place the sliced pumpkin in boiling salted water. Simmer until pumpkin is tender, about 15 to 20 minutes. Drain thoroughly.

Serving suggestion
Serve as an accompaniment to any main course.

Serves 3 to 4

Breadfruit in Coconut Sauce

Caymen Islands

Ingredients
1 under-ripe breadfruit
600 ml/1 pint coconut milk
3 spring onions, chopped
1 tomato, skinned and chopped
4 slices hot red pepper, de-seeded
1 sprig thyme

Method
Sauté the tomato, hot pepper, spring onions and thyme in a large frying pan. Meanwhile, peel and slice the breadfruit. Add the coconut milk to the pan, bring to the boil then reduce the heat and add the breadfruit and salt and pepper to taste. Cover and simmer for about 30 minutes or until the breadfruit is tender.

Serving suggestion
Serve with rice.

Serves 4 to 5

Author's note: Use either canned coconut milk or half a block of creamed coconut mixed with a little water.

Breadfruit Porridge

St Kitts

Ingredients
170 g/6 oz ripe breadfruit, peeled and sliced
1 litre/1¾ pints milk
6 teaspoons brown sugar
1 teaspoon vanilla essence

Method
Pour 300 ml/10 fl oz of milk into a large saucepan and add the breadfruit slices. Simmer over a low heat for 5 to 7 minutes. Remove from heat, and add the remainder of the milk and the rest of the ingredients. Return to the heat and simmer, stirring constantly, for another 7 minutes or until the breadfruit is well cooked.

Serving suggestion
Serve hot on its own or with other dishes for breakfast.

Serves 4

Breadfruit Puffs

Grenada

Ingredients
1 breadfruit
1 medium onion, chopped
2 blades chives, chopped
230 g/8 oz fresh white breadcrumbs
1 egg, size 2, beaten
2 tablespoons unsalted butter
Vegetable oil for frying

Method
Peel and chop the breadfruit into bite-size pieces. Place in a saucepan of boiling water, reduce heat, and cook until tender, about 15 minutes, then drain. While still hot, mash with butter and combine with chives and freshly ground black pepper. Dip spoonfuls of the mixture into the beaten egg then roll in breadcrumbs and deep-fry until golden.

Serving suggestion
Serve hot with other snacks as an appetiser. Vegans should substitute beaten egg with soya milk.

Makes approximately 30 puffs

Calas

Curaçao

Ingredients
230 g/8 oz black eye peas
2 hot red peppers, de-seeded and chopped
1 clove garlic, crushed
2 teaspoons salt
Cooking oil for frying

Method
Soak the peas overnight in enough cold water to cover them. Next day, drain and discard the water, rub off the skins, then cover again with cold water and leave for two hours. Afterwards, rinse and drain the peas, place in a processor and blend to a puree. Add the peppers and garlic and process for a few more seconds. Add the salt then turn out into a dish and beat with a wooden spoon until light and fluffy. Heat the oil in a heavy base frying pan or deep fat fryer until it is smoking. Drop tablespoons of the mixture into the hot oil, then fry for about two minutes, or until golden on both sides. When cooked, drain on kitchen paper.

Serving suggestion
Serve hot as a snack or appetiser.

Makes about 25

Candied Sweet Potatoes

Bahamas

Ingredients
680 g/1½ lb sweet potatoes
110 g/4 oz unsalted butter
110 g/4 oz brown sugar
1 tablespoon fresh lime juice
½ teaspoon freshly grated nutmeg
150 ml/5 fl oz water

Method
Wash the sweet potatoes then boil in the skins for 12 minutes or until almost tender. Meanwhile, make syrup of water, lime juice and sugar in a small saucepan. Cook until the syrup is thick and the sugar has dissolved, about 4 minutes. Butter a shallow baking dish. Peel the potatoes and cut them lengthways into ½ inch pieces. Lay the pieces in the baking dish and pour the syrup over. Grate the nutmeg on top and bake at gas mark 5, 375°F, 190°C, in the centre of the oven for 40 minutes, or until potatoes are browned.

Serving suggestion
Serve with mixed salad, roasted corn and callaloo.

Serves 4

Carrot Dumplings

Montserrat

Ingredients
60 g/2 oz finely grated carrot
80 g/3 oz plain flour
60 g/2 oz unsalted butter
1 teaspoon baking powder
½ teaspoon salt

Method
Sift the baking powder, flour and salt into a medium bowl. Rub in the butter with the fingertips until the mixture resembles fine breadcrumbs. Add the grated carrot and enough cold water - a few drops at a time - to form a stiff dough. Turn out onto a floured surface and shape into balls of about 1 inch diameter. Finally, drop into soup or simmering water and cook uncovered for 15 minutes. Serve hot.

Serving suggestion
These dumplings make a welcome addition to any vegetable soup. Or they can be served as a starter with a spinach, green pea or red or green pureed capsicum sauce.

Makes 14

Cassava Meal Dumplings

St Vincent

Ingredients
900 g/2 lb cassava meal
1 egg, size 1, well beaten
2 tablespoons unsalted butter
1 teaspoon salt
300 ml/10 fl oz water
Vegetable oil for frying
Freshly ground black pepper

Method
Place the cassava and water in a large saucepan on a low heat and stir constantly until the mixture turns clear. Allow to cool, then add the beaten egg, salt, pepper and butter. Heat the oil in a large frying pan then drop tablespoons of the mixture into the hot oil. Cook until golden brown on both sides, about 4 minutes on a medium heat. Drain and serve hot.

Serving suggestion
Serve with a side salad, boiled carrots and roasted corn.

Serves 4 to 6

Christophene (Cho-Cho) Salad

Haiti

Ingredients
900 g/2 lbs christophene (cho-cho)
450 g/1 lb firm, ripe tomatoes, sliced
3 shallots, thinly sliced
2 tablespoons fresh parsley, finely chopped

Dressing
3 teaspoons Dijon mustard
6 tablespoons extra virgin olive oil
3 tablespoons red wine vinegar
½ hot red pepper, de-seeded and finely chopped
2 teaspoons minced garlic

Method
Cut the christophene into 5 cm/2-inch strips and steam for 4 to 5 minutes or until tender, then allow to cool. Meanwhile, place all the ingredients for the dressing into a blender or screw-top jar and blend or shake until the ingredients are well mixed. Arrange the christophene and the other salad ingredients in a bowl or dish and garnish with chopped parsley. Cover and place in the refrigerator for two hours. Just before serving, pour the dressing over the salad.

Serving suggestion
This is a versatile salad which can be served with a wide variety of dishes.

Serves 4 to 5 as a side dish

Coo-Coo

Barbados

Ingredients
12 small okras, topped and tailed and cut into rounds
230 g/8 oz yellow cornmeal
60 g/2 oz unsalted butter
1.4 litres/2½ pints water
Freshly ground black pepper
Salt

Method
Bring the water to the boil in a large saucepan, add salt and okras and cook covered for ten minutes. Pour the cornmeal into the saucepan in a slow steady stream, stirring constantly with a wooden spoon. Cook for a further 5 minutes, making sure that all lumps have been removed and the mixture has thickened. This is best achieved over a low heat. Turn out onto a warm serving dish and pour melted butter over the top and season with more salt and pepper.

Serving suggestion
Serve hot as a main course.

Serves 4 as a main course and 6 as a side dish

Cornmeal and Cheese Cakes

Mustique

Ingredients
170 g/6 oz cornmeal
110 g/4 oz grated cheese
725 ml/1¼ pints water
1 teaspoon salt
Cooking oil for frying

Method
Bring 600 ml/1 pint of water to the boil. Moisten cornmeal with the remaining 150 ml/5 fl oz of water and add salt. Place in the boiled water and stir constantly until mixture is thick. Add grated cheese and allow to cool. Shape into round cakes about ½ inch thick and 5 cm/2 inches in diameter, then fry in hot oil, drain and serve hot.

Serving suggestion
Serve on its own as a snack or as part of a breakfast or brunch with fried plantain.

Makes 12 cakes

Creme de Christophene

Dominica

Ingredients
6 medium christophenes (cho-cho)
1 medium onion, thinly sliced
300 ml/10 fl oz milk
3 teaspoons arrowroot
1 clove garlic, crushed
60 g/2 oz unsalted butter
2 tablespoons cooking oil
Freshly ground black pepper
Salt

Method
Peel and thinly slice the christophenes and place in a large saucepan and cover with water. Cook over a low heat for 15 minutes, drain and then lay slices in a shallow baking dish. Make a thick white sauce (see page 282). Fry onions in cooking oil until the onion has softened but not browned. Transfer onion to sauce, combine and then spoon over christophene. Brown under a grill for a few minutes, and allow to cool before serving.

Serving suggestion
Serve with rice, boiled corn and fried plantain.

Serves 8

Curried Ackees

Jamaica

Ingredients
2 tins ackee (outside of Jamaica and Trinidad it is difficult to obtain fresh ackees)
2 medium onions, finely chopped
2 small tomatoes, skinned and chopped
2 tablespoons curry powder
1 tablespoon cooking oil
Freshly ground black pepper
Salt

Method
Sauté the onions and tomatoes in a frying pan. Cook until the onion has softened and is translucent. Stir in the curry powder and cook for a further 2 minutes over a low heat. Drain the tinned ackees and add to the pan. Stir and heat through, taking care not to break up the ackees too much.

Serving suggestion
Serve hot with rice and peas or plain boiled rice and a side salad as a main course. This mixture makes an ideal filling for patties.

Serves 4 to 6

Dhal

Trinidad

Ingredients
450 g/1 lb split peas or brown lentils
1 medium onion, finely chopped
2 cloves garlic, chopped
1½ teaspoons cumin seeds
1½ teaspoons turmeric
2 teaspoons coconut oil or ghee
900 ml/1½ pints water

Method
Soak the peas/lentils overnight, then drain and place in a large pan or pressure cooker with the water, turmeric and cumin and cook covered for 1 hour or until peas are tender. Sauté the garlic and onion in a frying pan until the onion is translucent. Strain the oil from the frying pan into the boiled peas/lentils. Season with salt and pepper, stir and cover and leave to stand for a few minutes before serving.

Serving suggestion
Serve with boiled rice or with roti, or as a side dish with a main course.

Serves 6 to 8

Author's note: The dhal should not be too watery, but if it is, reduce the excess liquid by cooking rapidly over a high heat.

Doubles (Bara and Curried Channa)

Trinidad

Ingredients
To make the baras
280 g/10 oz flour
1 teaspoon saffron powder
½ teaspoon ground cumin
1 teaspoon yeast
½ teaspoon salt
¼ teaspoon sugar
90 ml/3 fl oz warm water
Oil for frying
Water

To make the filling
230 g/8 oz channa (soaked overnight)
1½ teaspoons curry powder
1 onion, sliced
3 cloves garlic, crushed
1 hot pepper
Pinch ground cumin
Pepper sauce
1 tablespoon corn oil
Salt to taste

Method
Combine the flour, saffron, cumin and salt in a large bowl.
Put the warm water, yeast and sugar in a small bowl and leave
to stand for about 5 minutes until ingredients have dissolved.
Then add the yeast mixture to the flour and enough water to

make a firm dough. Cover with a damp cloth and leave to rise for about 1½ hours. Boil the channa with salt and ½ tablespoon of curry powder until tender, then drain. Heat oil in a heavy iron pot and saute the garlic, onion, remaining curry powder and a little water for a few minutes. Add the channa, stir well and cook for 5 minutes. Add 300 ml/10 fl oz water, cumin, salt, pepper and cover, lower the heat and simmer until peas are very soft. Add more water if necessary, and salt to taste. Knead the dough and leave to stand for a further 10-15 minutes. Take a tablespoon of dough and use both hands to flatten to about ¼ inch thick, then fry on both sides and drain on kitchen paper. To make the doubles, place 2 tablespoons of channa on one bara and cover with another, like a sandwich.

Serving suggestion

This is a complete snack meal which only requires pepper sauce or mango chutney.

Eggplant Chokha

Trinidad

Ingredients
1 large eggplant (aubergine)
2 cloves garlic
1 onion, chopped
Salt and freshly ground black pepper

Method
Wash and dry the eggplant and lightly coat it with cooking oil. Push the cloves of garlic into the eggplant and bake at gas mark 4, 350°F, 180°C, until tender. Then cut in half and scoop out the flesh. Mix with the chopped onion and mashed baked garlic, and season with salt and pepper. Serve hot.

Serving suggestion
Serve as a side dish or with roti.

Eggplant Creole

Dominica

Ingredients
3 large eggplants (aubergines)
2 green capsicums, de-seeded and diced
2 medium onions, sliced
1 large tomato, skinned and chopped
1 clove garlic, crushed
2 tablespoons tomato puree
2 tablespoons unsalted butter
½ teaspoon sugar
Dash of hot pepper sauce

Method
Slice the eggplants very thinly and boil in salt water until tender, about 10 minutes. Drain and set aside. Sauté the onions, tomato and capsicum in the butter in a shallow frying pan. Add crushed garlic and sauté on a low heat for a further 5 minutes. Add tomato puree, salt and pepper, plus 60 ml/2 fl oz of water. Simmer for 4 minutes. Add the slices of eggplant, warm through, and serve.

Serving suggestion
Serve with sautéed potatoes, fried plantain and plain boiled rice.

Serves 4 as a side dish

Gado Gado

Surinam

Ingredients
450 g/1 lb green beans, topped and tailed and chopped into
2.5 cm/1-inch pieces
450 g/1 lb potatoes, peeled and quartered
1 white cabbage, shredded
1 lettuce
1 cucumber
1 tomato, finely sliced
110 g/4 oz bean sprouts
2 eggs, hard-boiled and finely sliced

Method
Simmer the cabbage and beans in salted boiling water for 5 minutes, drain and reserve. Boil potatoes in salted water and cook for 20 minutes or until tender. Next, slice the cucumber and shred the lettuce and place in a salad dish. Soak the bean sprouts in water for 10 minutes then stir-fry for 2 minutes and allow to cool. Then lay the bean sprouts on top of the cucumber and lettuce. Put the boiled potatoes, cabbage and beans on next and garnish with sliced tomato and egg slices.

Serving suggestion
Serve hot or cold as a first course or as part of a larger meal with peanut sauce.

Serves 4 to 6

Green Plantain Chips

Cuba

Ingredients
2 large green plantains, peeled and cut into 2.5 cm/1-inch slices
Cooking oil for frying
Salt

Method
Place the sliced plantain in cold water and leave for 1 hour. Drain then salt the slices and leave to drain in a colander for 30 minutes. Rinse and drain, then dry on kitchen paper. Heat 6 tablespoons of oil in a heavy base frying pan and sauté the plantain pieces until tender - do not brown - and drain on kitchen paper. Place the plantain between two pieces of grease-proof paper and flatten with a rolling pin, until they are ½ inch thick. Then dip in salted water and fry again until they are golden brown on both sides, about 2 minutes.

Serving suggestion
Serve with salad or with drinks.

Makes about 30

Classic Caribbean Cooking

Grilled Corn on the Cob

Jamaica

Ingredients
4 young corn on the cob
Extra virgin olive oil
Butter
Salt and freshly ground black pepper

Method
Strip the corn, brush with olive oil and place under a moderately hot grill. Turn frequently until the corn has swollen and slightly blackened, then remove, add salt, pepper and melted butter.

Serving suggestion
Serve as a starter or side dish.

Serves 4

Limed Melongene

Guyana

Ingredients
3 medium melongenes (aubergines)
150 ml/5 fl oz extra virgin olive oil
Juice of 4 freshly squeezed limes
Salt

Method
Slice the melongenes into ¼ inch slices, salt and pour lime juice over. Leave to marinate for 1 hour. Without washing or wiping, fry the slices on both sides in hot olive oil until the slices are crisping at the edges and just beginning to brown.

Serving Suggestion
Serve on its own as a snack or with rice and roti.

Serves 4

Okra in Tomato Sauce

US Virgin Islands

Ingredients
450 g/1 lb okras
4 medium tomatoes, skinned and chopped
1 medium onion, chopped
1 scotch bonnet pepper, de-seeded and chopped
1 clove garlic, crushed
Salt and freshly ground black pepper
Pinch of sugar
Cooking oil

Method
Wash and top and tail the okras. Sauté the onions, garlic and okras in a frying pan with a lid. When okra is lightly brown add the tomatoes, sugar, salt and pepper, stir well, then cover and cook for about 4 minutes. Serve hot or cold.

Serving suggestion
Serve with rice and candied sweet potato.

Serves 6

Orange Green Beans

Guadeloupe

Ingredients
680 g/1½ lb whole green beans
2 tablespoons freshly squeezed and strained orange juice
2 teaspoons freshly squeezed lime juice
1 teaspoon grated orange rind
½ teaspoon crushed garlic
¼ teaspoon ground ginger
2 tablespoons extra virgin olive oil
Dash of hot pepper sauce
Salt to taste

Method
Place beans in a steamer or saucepan with just enough water to cover. Cook until tender but still crisp. Re-fresh under cold running water, then drain. Meanwhile, place the remainder of the ingredients in a blender or screw top jar, and mix until all the ingredients are well combined. Return beans to the steamer and heat through, then pour dressing over, cool slightly, then refrigerate covered for 3 hours, stirring occasionally.

Serving suggestion
Serve cold as part of a salad, garnished with sliced oranges, or with plain boiled rice or rice and peas, okra in tomato and fried plantain.

Serves 4

Palm Heart Fritters

Guadeloupe

Ingredients
1 large can palm hearts
1 medium onion, finely chopped
1 hot red pepper, de-seeded and finely chopped
1 clove garlic, minced
2 eggs, size 2, lightly beaten
110 g/4 oz plain flour
1 tablespoon freshly chopped parsley
1 teaspoon baking powder
Freshly ground black pepper
1 teaspoon salt
Cooking oil for deep frying

Method
Sift the flour, baking powder and salt into a large bowl. Then stir in the eggs with a little milk and water to make a mixture which is the consistency of a stiffish dough. Add onion, garlic, chopped palm hearts, red pepper, parsley, salt and pepper, and mix well, then leave to stand for an hour. Then shape tablespoon-sized portions of the mixture and deep fry, one at a time, until golden brown. Remove and drain on kitchen paper, keep hot until all are cooked.

Serving suggestion
Serve with a fresh tomato sauce as an accompaniment to a main course, or with rice, potatoes and salad as a main course.

Serves 6

Palm Hearts in Tomato Sauce

Martinique

Ingredients
2 tins palm hearts
300 ml/10 fl oz freshly made tomato sauce
60 g/2 oz freshly grated parmesan or other hard, strong cheese
30 g/1 oz parsley, freshly chopped

Method
Cut the palm hearts lengthways and place them in a shallow, oven-proof dish. Spoon over fresh tomato sauce, then sprinkle cheese on top and place under a pre-heated hot grill to brown. This should take about 4 to 5 minutes. Serve garnished with parsley.

Serving suggestion
Serve with plain boiled rice and callaloo.

Serves 6 as a main course

Paw-Paw au Gratin

Dominica

Ingredients

1 medium green paw-paw, peeled, de-seeded and sliced
1 medium onion, chopped
1 clove garlic, crushed
3 teaspoons arrowroot, mixed with water to a milk-like consistency
300 ml/10 fl oz milk
110 g/4 oz strong, hard cheese, grated

110 g/4 oz fresh white breadcrumbs
2 tablespoons unsalted butter
Salt and freshly ground black pepper
Cooking oil
1 teaspoon English mustard

Method

Place the sliced paw-paw in a pan of cold water, bring to the boil, then turn down and boil for about twenty minutes or until soft. Drain and mash the paw-paw and add a tablespoon of unsalted butter, salt and pepper. Sauté the garlic and onion until soft. Melt a tablespoon of butter in a saucepan, add the mustard and milk, and bring to the boil. Remove from the heat and add the grated cheese and arrow root, stirring constantly until the cheese has melted and the sauce has thickened. Allow to cool. Butter a gratin dish or a shallow oven-proof baking dish. Mix the paw-paw into the sauce and place in the dish. Sprinkle breadcrumbs on top and brown under a pre-heated hot grill for a few minutes.

Serving suggestion

Serve hot with fried or steamed rice or potatoes, and a green vegetable and salad.

Serves 4

Potato Curry

Guyana

Ingredients
450 g/1 lb old potatoes, peeled and sliced
230 g/8 oz tomatoes, skinned, chopped and de-seeded
1 medium onion, chopped
1 clove garlic, crushed
30/1 oz creamed coconut or coconut milk
3 tablespoons cooking oil or ghee
2 tablespoons curry powder (see page 292)
1 tablespoon tamarind paste
Salt and freshly ground black pepper

Method
Sauté the onion and garlic in cooking oil or ghee until the onion is soft, then add curry powder and tamarind paste and cook for a further 2 to 3 minutes. Add potatoes and tomatoes and cook gently over a low heat until the potatoes are soft, about 15 minutes. Finally, add the creamed coconut or coconut milk and a little water if using the creamed coconut. Serve hot when the coconut has been absorbed.

Serving suggestion
This is an ideal filling for a vegetarian roti, or serve with rice and salad.

Serves 4 as a side dish, or will make about six rotis

Pumpkin Curry

Guadeloupe

Ingredients
450 g/1 lb pumpkin, peeled, de-seeded and diced
3 medium ripe tomatoes, skinned and chopped
1 green capsicum, de-seeded and chopped
1 small onion, finely chopped
2 cloves garlic, crushed
1 tablespoon curry powder
2 tablespoons unsalted butter
3 tablespoons cooking oil
Salt and freshly ground white pepper

Method
Heat the oil and butter in a heavy base saucepan or casserole, sweat the onions for about 2 minutes with the lid on, then add the curry powder and pepper and stir well. Next, add the diced pumpkin, tomatoes and salt, and reduce the heat. Stir the mixture from time to time to prevent it sticking. When almost cooked, about 20 minutes, add the garlic. The pumpkin should be tender, but if you like a more mushy consistency, cook for longer.

Serving suggestion
Serve as a main course with boiled rice, mango chutney and a salad, or as an accompaniment to other dishes.

Serves 6 as a main course

Pumpkin Pancake

Martinique

Ingredients
230 g/8 oz pumpkin
30 g/1 oz plain flour
1 egg, size 2
1 tablespoon caster sugar
½ teaspoon baking powder
¼ teaspoon mixed spice

Method
Wash and peel the pumpkin, cut into cubes, and steam for 15 minutes or until soft. Mash the pumpkin, then stir in all the other ingredients, and beat well. Fry desert spoonfuls in smoking hot oil for about 2 minutes over a moderate heat. Drain on kitchen paper.

Serving suggestion
Serve hot, sprinkled with sugar, as a snack.

Serves 4

Rice and Raisin Croquettes

Tobago

Ingredients

60 g/2 oz long grain rice
300 ml/10 fl oz milk
60 g/2 oz butter
30 g/1 oz raisins
Yolk 2 eggs, size 2
1 small onion, peeled and
stuck with 8 cloves

Fresh white breadcrumbs
Plain flour
600 ml/1 pint water
Salt and freshly ground
black pepper

Method

Boil milk with onion, butter and salt, for 2 minutes in a medium saucepan. Then bring the rice to the boil and cook for 3 minutes. Drain the rice and combine with the milk in an oven-proof dish and bake in the oven at gas mark 3, 325°F, 160°C, for 30 minutes. Remove the onion from the rice dish using a slotted spoon. Mix 10 g/½ oz of butter with the egg yolks and 1 tablespoon of milk. Retain a quarter of the yolk mixture and pour the rest into the rice and add the raisins. Set aside to get cold. Once cold, cut out rectangular shapes of the rice mixture (about 1 inch thick), dip into egg mixture, roll in breadcrumbs and fry in the remaining butter until the croquettes are golden brown on all sides.

Serving suggestion

Serve with salad.

Serves 4 to 6 as a side dish

Spicy Okra

Guyana

Ingredients
450 g/1 lb okra, topped and tailed, and cut into ½ inch pieces
1 large onion, peeled and sliced
2 cloves garlic, peeled and sliced
3 tablespoons ghee or vegetable oil
1 tablespoon ground coriander
1 teaspoon freshly ground black pepper
1 teaspoon ground turmeric
½ teaspoon garam masala
½ teaspoon salt
600 ml/1 pint water

Method
Melt the ghee in a cast iron or heavy frying pan, on a low heat and add the onions and garlic and cook until soft, without caramelising. Then add all the other ingredients - except the okra, garam masala and water - and fry for another 4 minutes, stirring constantly. Then add the okra, coat with the mixture, and then stir in the water. Cover and simmer for 5 to 10 minutes or until the okra is tender. Stir in the garam masala, then remove from heat and serve.

Serving suggestion
Serve with plain boiled rice and roti.

Serves 4

Split Pea Fritters (Phulouri)

Trinidad and Tobago

Ingredients
230 g/8 oz split peas
1 medium onion, chopped
1 clove garlic, chopped
Salt and freshly ground black pepper
Cooking oil for deep frying

Method
Soak the peas overnight in cold water. Drain and then place in a blender or food processor with the chopped onion and garlic, and blend into a puree. Use a tablespoon to shape the mixture into flattened balls and deep fry four or six at a time in hot oil. When the fritters are brown on both sides they are done. Remove and drain on kitchen paper.

Serving suggestion
Serve hot with a pepper sauce, tomato sauce or mango chutney.

Makes 24

Stewed Cucumbers in Orange Sauce

Puerto Rico

Ingredients
4 cucumbers, 6 to 8 inches long
300 ml/10 fl oz freshly squeezed orange juice
60 g/2 oz unsalted butter
1 tablespoon arrowroot
1 teaspoon freshly grated orange rind
1 pint salted water
Salt and freshly ground white pepper

Method
Peel and split the cucumbers lengthways, de-seed and cut into ½-inch segments. Melt the butter in a small a saucepan, add the arrowroot and mix to a smooth paste. Next, add the strained orange juice, orange rind, salt and pepper, and stir constantly until thickened. In another large pan, bring the salted water to the boil, add the cucumbers and simmer for 5 minutes. Drain and place on a dish, then pour sauce over cucumbers.

Serving suggestion
Serve hot or cold as an accompaniment to any main course, or with boiled callaloo and rice.

Serves 4

Vegetable Oven Omelette

Nevis

Ingredients
6 eggs, size 2
110 g/4 oz cheese, grated
230 g/8 oz chopped broccoli
1 medium onion, finely chopped
1 medium tomato, cut into six slices
¼ teaspoon garlic powder
2 tablespoons milk
Salt and freshly ground black pepper

Method
Beat eggs with a whisk until they become light and fluffy. Stir in broccoli, onion, milk, salt, garlic powder and the majority of the grated cheese. Pour mixture into an un-greased baking dish, arrange sliced tomatoes on top and then cover with the remainder of the cheese. Cook at gas mark 3, 325°F, 160°C, for 20 to 25 minutes or until egg is set.

Serving suggestion
Serve with fried potatoes and a green salad.

Serves 6

Yam Puffs

Grenada

Ingredients
450 g/1 lb yams
4 eggs, size 2
2 tablespoons unsalted butter
Pinch of salt

Method
Peel, wash and slice the yam. Boil in salted water until tender.
Drain and mash with butter and freshly ground black pepper
while still hot. Add eggs to the yam mixture and beat well.
Then drop desert spoonfuls into hot oil and remove when puffs
float to the top and are golden brown.

Serving suggestion
Serve hot as a snack.

Serves 4 to 6

Game

Braised Duck

Jamaica

Ingredients
1.8 kg/4 lb duckling
1.2 litres/2 pints groundnut oil
600 ml/1 pint good chicken stock
1 medium onion, peeled and sliced
4 tablespoons dry sherry or Chinese rice wine
4 tablespoons dark soy sauce
4 tablespoons freshly squeezed orange juice
1 tablespoon malt vinegar
2 slices fresh ginger
4 teaspoons salt
½ teaspoon five spice powder

Method
Place the duck in a large pan of boiling water and leave for 2 minutes, then drain and pat dry with kitchen paper. In a Dutch oven or large heavy pot place all the ingredients, except the oil. Bring to the boil, then place the duck in the pot and cover with a tight fitting lid. Simmer on a low heat for 45 minutes, turning the duck at least 4 times during cooking. Then remove duck, drain well and dry. The cooking liquid should be left uncovered on the heat to reduce and thicken. Then, heat the oil in a wok or large deep fat fryer and cook the duck until it has browned. Lift out then chop into bite size pieces and return to the sauce to coat the meat. Remove to a large platter and serve hot.

Serving suggestion
Serve with the remainder of the sauce handed separately, and plain boiled rice or deep-fried noodles.

Serves 4 as a main course or 6 to 8 as part of a Chinese banquet

Braised Rabbit in Molasses

Jamaica

Ingredients
900 g/2 lbs jointed rabbit
1 scotch bonnet pepper, de-seeded and finely sliced
1 medium onion, finely chopped
2 cloves garlic, crushed
90 ml/3 fl oz molasses
60 ml/2 fl oz white wine vinegar
180 ml/6 fl oz water
2 teaspoons salt

Method
Season rabbit with salt, pepper and one clove of crushed garlic. Place in a large cast iron pot or Dutch oven and pour over vinegar, water and molasses. Sauté the onion and remaining garlic in a frying pan and add to the pot. Bring to the boil and stir, add the scotch bonnet pepper and cover. Simmer for 2 hours or until rabbit is tender and well browned, basting periodically. Serve hot.

Serving suggestion
Serve with rice, fried green bananas and an avocado, tomato and onion salad.

Serves 6 to 8

Curried Rabbit

St Kitts

Ingredients
1.3 kg/3 lbs jointed rabbit
300 ml/10 fl oz chicken or rabbit stock
300 ml/10 fl oz coconut milk
3 medium onions, finely chopped
3 tablespoons unsalted butter
3 tablespoons guava jelly
3 tablespoons freshly squeezed lime juice
3 tablespoons curry powder
3 teaspoons arrowroot

Method
Season rabbit with salt and pepper and then fry in butter in a large frying pan until brown on all sides. Transfer the rabbit pieces to a large heavy cooking pot or casserole. Then sauté the onions until softened and golden, add the curry powder and cook for a further 2 minutes. Add the stock and coconut milk and bring to the boil. Pour this sauce mixture into the cooking pot with the rabbit, stir in the guava jelly and bring to the boil. Cover and simmer for 2 hours or until rabbit is tender. Finally, add the arrowroot mixed with the lime juice and cook for another three minutes or until sauce has thickened. Serve hot.

Serving suggestion
Serve with rice and some chutney.

Serves 5 to 6

Duck in Rum

Martinique

Ingredients
2.3 kg/5 lb Barbary duck
300 ml/10 fl oz stock, made from duck giblets or chicken stock
1 slice streaky bacon
2 medium onions, finely chopped
2 cloves garlic, finely chopped
1 stick celery, finely sliced
3 sprigs fresh parsley
3 sprigs thyme
1 fresh bay leaf
1 sprig fresh sage
90 ml/3 fl oz dark rum
30 g/1 oz unsalted butter
Salt and freshly ground black pepper

Method
Tie the herbs together, then add the butter to a casserole or Dutch oven and sauté the duck until brown. Next, sauté the garlic and onion, until soft. Discard the fat then add the herbs, celery and stock. Bring to the boil then simmer for 1½ hours or until tender. Add pepper and chopped grilled bacon and cook over a low heat for another 15 minutes. Heat the rum in a metal ladle held over the flame then set alight (take care, a long taper is safest for this procedure). When flames subside, pour over duck, then joint and serve.

Serving suggestion
Serve with rice and sauce poured over a salad of watercress avocado and orange goes well with this dish.

Serves 6

Miscellaneous

Escargots (Snails)

Guadeloupe

Ingredients
24 snails
300 ml/10 fl oz double cream
230 g/8 oz finely chopped callaloo
2 large onions, finely chopped
2 hot red peppers, de-seeded and finely chopped
3 cloves garlic, finely chopped
1.4 litres/2½ pints water
Freshly ground black pepper
Salt

Method
Put water in a large saucepan, add salt and bring to the boil. Add the snails and cook for 30 minutes. Drain and remove snails from shells with a fork or lobster pick. Remove entrails from the backs of the snails by cutting a thin line the length of the snail and remove under running water. Rinse and cut each snail in half, then set aside. In a medium saucepan melt butter then sauté the peppers, garlic and onion for about 10 minutes. Next, add the snails and callaloo and stir constantly for 5 minutes. Then add the cream and black pepper and cook on a low heat for a further 10 minutes. Do not allow to boil as the cream will curdle.

Serving suggestion
Serve on a bed of plain boiled white rice.

Serves 4

Fricassee Crapaud (Frog)

Dominica

Ingredients
3 frogs
1 medium onion, chopped
1 stick celery, chopped
1 clove garlic, crushed
3 cloves
60 g/2 oz unsalted butter
60 g/2 oz plain flour
1 tablespoon tomato paste
2 teaspoons white wine vinegar
Juice of one lime
150 ml/5 fl oz cooking oil
360 ml/12 fl oz cold water
Freshly ground black pepper

Method
Clean and joint frogs and wash with lime juice. Season with a teaspoon of vinegar, salt, pepper, chopped onion, celery and garlic, and leave for 1 hour. Next, remove seasonings and dry the meat with kitchen paper, then roll each piece in flour, and fry until golden brown on a moderate heat. Sauté the seasonings in the remainder of the oil. Melt the butter in a large pot, add sautéed seasonings and fried meat, then add water. Simmer for 5 minutes, then add tomato paste, vinegar and salt and pepper to taste and simmer for a further 5 to 7 minutes. If sauce is too watery, thicken with a little arrowroot.

Serves 4 as a main course

Tripe and Beans

St Kitts

Ingredients
900 g/2 lb tripe
450 g/1 lb cooked butter beans
3 medium tomatoes, skinned and chopped
3 medium onions, finely chopped
5 slices hot red pepper, de-seeded
1 sprig thyme, chopped
1 clove garlic, crushed
3 tablespoons curry powder
Salt and freshly ground black pepper

Method
Wash and thoroughly clean the tripe. Cut into bite-size pieces and place in a saucepan with enough water to cover. Bring to the boil then simmer covered for 2½ hours or until tender. Add the remaining ingredients, except the butter beans, cover and simmer for a further 5 minutes. Add butter beans and cook for another 5 minutes or until sauce is thick.

Serving suggestion
Serve with bread for a light lunch or with rice and yam for a more substantial meal.

Serves 4

Classic Caribbean Cooking

Turtle Stew

Cayman Islands

Ingredients
900 g/2 lb turtle meat (see Author's note)
4 large tomatoes, skinned and chopped
1 large onion
12 cloves
3 sprigs parsley
2 sprigs thyme
½ tablespoon arrowroot paste
2.5 cm/1 inch cinnamon bark
1 pinch nutmeg
½ glass dry sherry
Juice of one large lime
4.5 litres/8 pints water

Method
Wash the turtle meat in water with the lime juice and place in a large pot. Add the water, onion, parsley, nutmeg, cloves, thyme and tomatoes and cook covered for 2½–3 hours. Top up with water if too much evaporates. Add sherry and a little arrowroot paste to thicken the stew about 15 minutes before the end of cooking.

Serving suggestion
Serve hot with boiled dumplings and garnished with tomato and lime wedges.

Serves 5 to 7

Author's note: The turtle is an endangered and protected species and this recipe has been included for historical reference.

Rice

Cook-up Rice

Dominica

Ingredients
680 g/1½ lb chicken back and neck (or pieces you prefer)
110 g/4 oz salt beef, cubed
450 g/1 lb long grain white rice
230 g/8 oz pigeon (gungo) peas
1 small coconut
2 medium onions, chopped
1 large tomato, chopped
2 bundles chives, chopped
2 tablespoons cooking oil
Freshly ground black pepper
Salt

Method
Soak the pigeon peas in cold water overnight. Season the chicken with chives, onions, tomato, salt and pepper and leave for 1 hour. Grate the coconut flesh, extract the milk and mix with 1 pint of water. Bring 1.4 litres/2½ pints of water to the boil and add the peas and cook for about an hour or until peas are soft. Brown the beef and chicken then place all the meat, seasonings and oil into a large pot, stir in the rice and coconut milk and finally add the peas. Cook for 20 minutes on a low heat until all the fluid has been absorbed and the rice and meat are tender. Serve as a complete meal.

Serves 4 to 6

Fried Rice Chow Fan

Trinidad

Ingredients
230 g/8 oz cooked shrimp, lobster and chicken
450 g/1 lb rice
2 eggs, size 2, lightly beaten
4 tablespoons chopped spring onions
3 tablespoons chopped parsley
Soy sauce
4 tablespoons cooking oil
Freshly ground black pepper
Salt
Water

Method
Cook rice in plenty of salted water, drain and refrigerate for 12 hours. Then heat oil in a wok and add the rice, stirring all the time until golden brown. Add chicken, lobster and shrimp and cook for 1 minute. Make a well in the centre of the rice and pour in the beaten eggs. Cook until eggs begin to set then add pepper, soy sauce, spring onions and parsley and stir well, breaking up the egg. Serve hot.

Serves 4 to 6 as a light meal

Rice and Peas

Jamaica

Ingredients
450 g/1 lb long grain white rice
230 g/8 oz gungo peas
600 ml/1 pint coconut milk
3 spring onions, finely chopped
3 sprigs thyme
1 clove garlic, chopped
1 tablespoon tomato paste
1 teaspoon sugar
600 ml/1 pint water

Method
Soak the peas in cold water overnight then drain and put into a large pot. Cover with water and bring to the boil, then reduce heat and add the sugar, spring onions, garlic, thyme and tomato paste and simmer for 2 hours. Then add the coconut milk and bring back to the boil. When the peas are almost tender, add the rice and salt to taste. Leave covered until the rice has absorbed all the liquid. Remove from the heat and leave covered for a further ten minutes before serving.

Serving suggestion
Rice and Peas is a popular accompaniment to almost any dish.

Serves 6 to 8

Author's note: Some cooks substitute red kidney beans for the gungo peas, or add peppers or even salt pork.

Seasoned Rice

Antigua

Ingredients

450 g/1 lb chicken, jointed
230 g/8 oz salt beef
450 g/1 lb easy-cook or long grain white rice
230 g/8 oz West Indian pumpkin, peeled and cubed
230 g/8 oz red peas, soaked overnight
1 large tomato, de-seeded and chopped
1 red capsicum, de-seeded and chopped
1 large onion, chopped
3 spring onions, chopped
½ hot red pepper, de-seeded and chopped
3 cloves garlic, finely chopped
2 sprigs fresh thyme leaves
2 tablespoons dark soy sauce
2 tablespoons unsalted butter
2 tablespoons cooking oil

Method

Place the salt beef in a large bowl, cover with cold water and leave for 1 hour then drain. Place the peas in a saucepan, cover with cold water and boil rapidly for 10 minutes, then drain and set aside. Heat the oil in a large cast iron or heavy frying pan with a lid, and brown the chicken for 5 minutes. Add the beef, garlic, onions, capsicum, thyme, pepper and pumpkin, and sauté for 2 minutes. Add the rice, tomato, salt and pepper, butter and soy sauce and cook for 4 minutes. Transfer all the ingredients to a large pot and cover with water. Bring to the boil, then reduce the heat and simmer for 30 minutes or until all the water has been absorbed and the peas are tender. Serve hot as a complete meal.

Serves 5 to 6

Soup

Ackee Soup

Jamaica

Ingredients
2 tins ackee, drained and mashed
230 g/8 oz salted pig's tail
2 spring onions, chopped
4 slices scotch bonnet pepper, de-seeded
1 sprig thyme
Freshly ground black pepper
Water

Method
Place the pig's tail, thyme, pepper, spring onions and black pepper in a large saucepan and cover with water. Boil for 5 minutes then simmer for 1 hour or until meat is tender. Add the mashed ackee to the soup and heat until piping hot. Season to taste and serve.

Serves 4

Beef Soup

Haiti

Ingredients
900 g/2 lb shin of beef
230 g/8 oz cubed salt beef
680 g/1½ lb West Indian pumpkin, peeled and diced
230 g/8 oz yam, peeled and diced
230 g/8 oz breadfruit, peeled and diced
3 carrots, peeled and diced
1 christophene, peeled and sliced
1 large onion, chopped
1 whole hot pepper
12 pimento (allspice) berries
1 clove garlic, crushed
3 sprigs thyme
450 g/1 lb plain flour (to make spinners)
2.8 litres/5 pints water

Method
Place the meats, carrots, christophene, pumpkin and hot pepper in a large pot or soup kettle, cover with water and bring to the boil, then cover and simmer for 2 hours. Meanwhile, make the spinners (see page 271) and add to the pot along with the breadfruit, yam, garlic, pimento, onion and thyme. Continue cooking until vegetables are tender, about 15 minutes. Remove pepper and serve.

Serving suggestion
This soup serves as a main course and requires no addition.

Serves 5 to 6

Beef Soup with Cabbage and Sweet Potato

Grenada

Ingredients
450 g/1 lb beef shin bones
450 g/1 lb lean beef
230 g/8 oz sweet potatoes, peeled and cubed
110 g/4 oz white cabbage, shredded
1 medium onion, finely chopped
2 sprigs parsley
2 sprigs thyme
1 fresh bay leaf
Salt and freshly ground black pepper

Method
In a large stock pot or saucepan place the shin bones, onion, bay leaf and 2.3 litres/4 pints of water. Bring to the boil then simmer for 1 hour skimming the surface occasionally. Then remove bay leaf and bones and boil rapidly until the stock has reduced to about 750 ml/1¼ pints. Add the cabbage, thyme and parsley and cook for a further 10 minutes. Finally, add the sweet potato and simmer for another 10 minutes or until the vegetables are tender, but not mushy. Season and serve hot.

Serving suggestion
This soup is filling and only needs bread to make it a main course.

Serves 4

Black Bean and Bacon Soup

Dominican Republic

Ingredients
450 g/1 lb gammon knuckle
450 g/1 lb dried black beans
450 g/1 lb onions, chopped
5 cloves garlic, chopped
6 tablespoons single cream
3 tablespoons soured cream
3 tablespoons rum
2 sprigs thyme
Freshly ground black pepper
Cold water

Method
Soak black beans overnight and then discard any beans that have floated to the top. Place gammon knuckle in a large basin, cover with cold water and leave for three hours. Rinse black beans in cold water then place in a large pot, cover with cold water and bring to the boil. Boil rapidly for 10 minutes then reduce the heat and simmer for 2 hours. Add the thyme, black pepper and onion and cover. Place the gammon knuckle in another large saucepan, cover with cold water and bring to the boil. Discard the water and repeat, then add the gammon to the bean soup. When the gammon is cooked, remove from the soup, flake off the meat and return to the soup. Stir in the rum (warmed) and the cream. Heat and serve garnished with a slice of hot pepper.

Serves 6

Black Bean Soup

Cuba

Ingredients
450 g/1 lb black beans, soaked overnight
2 small green capsicums, de-seeded and diced
2 small carrots, peeled and diced
1 large onion, finely chopped
2 stalks celery, diced
1 bunch chives, chopped (for the garnish)
4 cloves garlic, finely chopped
½ tablespoon cumin seeds
6 tablespoons extra virgin olive oil
1 tablespoon distilled white vinegar
3 teaspoons salt

Method
Place beans in cold water and simmer until soft. Meanwhile, sauté onion, peppers, carrots and celery until onion has caramelised. Add cumin, vinegar and garlic and cook and stir for 3 minutes. Remove about ½ pint of the bean water and add to the vegetables, then cook for 20 minutes on a low heat. Combine with beans, season to taste and add more water if the soup is too thick. Serve hot garnished with chopped chives.

Serves 8 to 10

Braf

Dominica

Ingredients
450 g/1 lb salted pork
450 g/1 lb sprats
450 g/1 lb green cabbage, shredded
230 g/8 oz dasheen, chopped
230 g/8 oz green bananas, peeled and chopped
230 g/8 oz tannias (see Glossary)
2 medium christophene, peeled and chopped
1 medium onion, peeled and chopped
1 hot pepper
3 cloves garlic, finely chopped
3 cloves
1 sprig thyme
Juice of 2 freshly squeezed limes
750 ml/1¼ pints water
Salt and black pepper to taste

Method
Soak meat in cold water for 1 hour to remove excess salt, then place in a pan with the water, bring to the boil, add onion, thyme, cloves, garlic, hot pepper and then reduce heat and simmer for 1½ hours or until meat is tender. Add the remaining ingredients and simmer for another 10 to 15 minutes to allow the vegetables to cook. Remove meat and chop into bite-size pieces. Return to the pan and serve hot. This complete meal requires no accompaniment.

Serves 6 to 8

Breadfruit Soup

Dominica

Ingredients
680 g/1½ lb breadfruit, cut into 1 inch cubes
450 g/1 lb beef soup bones (from butcher)
1 green capsicum, de-seeded and diced
1 small onion, finely chopped
1 stalk celery, diced
2 blades chives, chopped
1 sprig thyme
1.4 litres/2½ pints water
Salt and pepper to taste
Chopped parsley for garnish

Method
Place washed soup bones in a large pot with water and boil for 1 hour. Add breadfruit cubes and continue to cook for a further 20 minutes. Finally, add all the seasonings, reduce the heat and simmer for 10 minutes. Serve piping hot, garnished with chopped parsley.

Serves 4

Chicken and Melongene Soup

Guyana

Ingredients
450 g/1 lb chicken breasts, skinned and boned
1.4 litres/2½ pints chicken stock
680 g/1½ lb ripe tomatoes, skinned and chopped
450 g/1 lb melongene (aubergine), cut into ½ inch cubes, with skin left on
1 medium onion, peeled and chopped
1 hot red pepper, de-seeded and cut into rings
4 cloves garlic, peeled and chopped
3 sprigs thyme
Juice of 1 freshly squeezed lime
Salt and freshly ground black pepper

Method
Place the chicken stock, pepper, garlic and half the lime juice in a large heavy pan. Bring to the boil, then reduce the heat to a simmer and gently poach the chicken, about 10 minutes. Remove the chicken and cut into small cubes. When cold, place in a dish and pour the remainder of the lime juice over and leave to marinate for 10 minutes. Add the tomatoes and thyme to the stock and simmer for 10 minutes. Then add the melongene and simmer for a further 5 minutes. Return the marinated chicken with the marinade to the cooking pot and cook for a further 2 minutes. Serve hot, garnished with the pepper rings.

Serves 4

Chicken Soup

Bonaire

Ingredients
1.3 kg/3 lb whole boiling chicken
900 g/2 lb beef soup bones
450 g/1 lb onions, chopped
230 g/8 oz West Indian pumpkin, peeled, de-seeded and chopped
3 sweet potatoes, peeled and sliced
3 medium potatoes, peeled and sliced
3 medium tomatoes, skinned and chopped
2 whole green peppers
1 ripe plantain, peeled and sliced into ½ inch pieces
2 corn on the cob, cut in half
1 sprig thyme
110 g/4 oz gungo peas
2.3 g/4 pints water

Method
Place the whole chicken, water and soup bones into a large pan, cover and simmer for 30 minutes and bring to the boil. Add all the other ingredients and simmer for another 40 minutes or until the chicken and vegetables are tender. Discard the beef bones and joint the chicken into 8 pieces and return to the pan. Serve piping hot as a complete meal.

Serves 8

Chilled Avocado Soup

Cayman Islands

Ingredients
4 avocados, peeled and stoned
600 ml/1 pint milk
3 spring onions, finely chopped
2 tablespoons freshly squeezed lime juice
4 drops hot pepper sauce
Salt and freshly ground black pepper

Method
Place all the ingredients in a processor or blender and liquidise for about 2 minutes. Transfer mixture to a tureen or bowl and chill for at least 4 hours before serving.

Serves 4

Chilled Breadfruit Soup

Grenada

Ingredients
450 g/1 lb breadfruit, peeled, cored and diced
1.4 litres/2½ pints chicken stock
300 ml/10 fl oz single cream
2 medium onions, finely chopped
1 clove garlic, chopped
3 tablespoons unsalted butter
Parsley to garnish

Method
Sauté the garlic and onions in the butter until onions are translucent. Transfer to a large pot and add the stock and the breadfruit. Bring to the boil then simmer for 20 minutes, or until breadfruit is tender. Allow to cool then liquidise for 2 minutes. Stir in the cream and chill for at least 6 hours before serving. Garnish with chopped parsley.

Serves 6

Chilled Cucumber Soup

Barbados

Ingredients
680 g/1½ lb cucumber
1.2 litres/2 pints chicken or vegetable stock
300 ml/10 fl oz double cream
1 medium onion, finely chopped
1 tablespoon spring onions, finely chopped
2 teaspoons arrowroot
Salt and freshly ground white pepper

Method
Peel and cube the cucumbers, place in a large saucepan with the onion and stock, cover and simmer for 20 minutes. Allow to cool, then liquidise into a smooth puree. Strain and return to the saucepan, add salt and pepper. Mix the arrowroot with a little milk, add to the soup and stir until slightly thickened, but do not boil. Stir in the cream and leave to cool. Transfer to the refrigerator for at least 6 hours. Serve garnished with spring onion tops.

Serves 6 to 7

Chilled Prawn and Tomato Soup

St Lucia

Ingredients
340 g/12 oz peeled prawns or shrimps
600 ml/1 pint fresh fish stock
230 g/8 oz tomatoes, skinned and chopped
230 g/8 oz cucumber, peeled and diced
1 spring onion, sliced
4 slices lime
3 sprigs parsley
2 tablespoons freshly squeezed lime juice
1 teaspoon Dijon mustard
6 drops hot pepper sauce
1 teaspoon freshly ground black pepper
1 teaspoon ground sea salt

Method
Place all the ingredients, except the lime slices and parsley, into a large soup tureen or bowl. Chill for 3 hours then serve garnished with a slice of lime and parsley.

Serves 4

Author's note: This is a fabulous soup for those who do not have time to cook, particularly on warm summer days or nights.

Coconut Soup

Jamaica

Ingredients
450 g/1 lb shin of beef, chopped
600 ml/1 pint fresh coconut milk
2 cocos, chopped (see Glossary)
2 spring onions, chopped
2 slices de-seeded scotch bonnet pepper
1 sprig thyme
Salt and freshly ground white pepper
2.3 litres/4 pints water

Method
Place the meat and cocos in a large pan with the water and simmer for approximately 2 hours. When meat is tender, add scotch bonnet pepper, salt, white pepper, thyme and spring onion, and then add coconut milk and simmer for 10 minutes. Serve hot.

Serves 5

Coconut Soup

St Kitts

Ingredients
230 g/8 oz freshly grated coconut
1 litre/1¾ pints chicken stock
300 ml/10 fl oz double cream
2 tablespoons plain flour
2 tablespoons unsalted butter
Pinch salt and freshly ground white pepper

Method
Place the coconut and chicken stock in a large saucepan, cover and simmer for 30 minutes. Strain the mixture and press the coconut to extract all the liquid. Mix the flour and butter together to form a paste and add to the soup, bit by bit, stirring constantly until dissolved. Allow the soup to thicken slightly before adding the cream. Heat through and serve.

Serves 5 to 6

Cold Curried Cucumber Soup

Haiti

Ingredients
600 ml/1 pint vegetable or chicken stock
150 ml/5 fl oz single cream
2 large cucumbers
3 spring onions, finely sliced
2 tablespoons freshly squeezed lime juice
2 tablespoons fresh coriander
4 teaspoons curry powder
3 drops hot pepper sauce
2 teaspoons freshly ground black pepper
1 teaspoon salt

Method
Grate the cucumbers and finely mince the coriander, then place in a large bowl and add all the remaining ingredients and mix well. Chill in the refrigerator for at least 4 hours before serving. Garnish with a thin slice of cucumber.

Serves 4 to 6

Crab Soup

Barbados

Ingredients
230 g/8 oz flaked crab meat
750 ml/1¼ pints fish stock
600 ml/1 pint milk or single cream
2 hard boiled eggs, mashed
2 tablespoons unsalted butter
1 tablespoon cornflour
Juice and finely grated rind of a lime
Dash of Angostura Bitters
Dash of pepper sauce

Method
Place butter in a saucepan and melt, then combine with the cornflour and mix to form a smooth paste. Remove from the heat, add the lime juice and rind, fish stock, mashed eggs, milk and crab meat. Return to the heat and simmer for 10 minutes. Season with salt and pepper and stir in the bitters and pepper sauce. Serve hot.

Serves 6 to 7

Crapaud (Frog) Soup

Dominica

Ingredients
2 crapauds (frogs)
4 large potatoes, peeled and diced
4 carrots, peeled and diced
1 turnip
1 leek, chopped
1 stalk celery, chopped
1 small onion, finely chopped
1 clove garlic, crushed
5 cloves
30 g/1 oz thin macaroni
2 tablespoons unsalted butter
Salt and freshly ground black pepper

Method
Clean and cut up the crapauds and sprinkle with salt and pepper. Boil the carrots, potatoes, leek and celery in 1.2 litres/2 pints of water for 20 minutes, then add cloves, garlic, macaroni, crapauds and onion, and simmer for a further 20 minutes. Add salt and pepper to taste. Serve hot.

Serves 4 as a main course

Author's note: This variety of frog may be difficult to obtain outside Dominica. However, some fishmongers may be able to obtain similar varieties (see Glossary).

Creamed Red Snapper Soup

Jamaica

Ingredients

900 g/1 lb red snapper fillets
360 ml/12 fl oz fish stock
150 ml/5 fl oz double cream
110 g/4 oz yam, peeled and diced
1 large potato, peeled and diced
1 carrot, peeled and diced
2 spring onions, chopped
1 clove garlic, crushed
1 tablespoon chopped spring onion tops
1 tablespoon finely chopped parsley
60 g/2 oz unsalted butter
Dash hot pepper sauce
360 ml/12 fl oz cold water
Salt and pepper to taste

Method

Skin the fish and cut into 1 inch cubes. Sauté the spring onions, carrot, yam, potato and garlic in a large soup kettle or pot for 5 minutes over a low heat, then add half the fish and cook covered for a further minute. Add stock and water, bring to the boil and simmer for 20 minutes. Pour into a blender and process until mixture is smooth, then return to the pot. Add the remainder of the fish, parsley, spring onion tops and pepper sauce and bring to the boil, then cook uncovered on a low heat for five minutes. Finally, stir in the cream and heat through, taking care not to boil otherwise the cream will curdle.

Serves 4

Eggplant Soup

Trinidad and Tobago

Ingredients
450 g/1 lb eggplants (aubergines), peeled and diced
900 ml/1½ pints chicken stock (or vegetable stock)
300 ml/10 fl oz whipping cream
3 whole spring onions, chopped
1 medium onion, finely sliced
1 sprig thyme
110 g/4 oz unsalted butter
Salt and freshly ground black pepper

Method
Heat the butter in a frying pan and sauté the onion, spring onion and ¾ of the eggplant, and cook until eggplant is translucent. Transfer to a pot, add the stock, salt and pepper, and simmer for 15 minutes, or until eggplant is tender. Then liquidise to form a puree and return to the pot, then stir in the cream. Sauté the remainder of the diced eggplant in the frying pan and transfer to soup dishes, then pour the soup over and serve.

Serves 6

Fish Tea

Jamaica

Ingredients
900 g/2 lb red snapper heads
4 green bananas, peeled and diced
1 whole green scotch bonnet pepper
3 spring onions, chopped
1 tomato, skinned and diced
1 clove garlic, crushed
2 sprigs thyme
1.4 litres/2½ pints cold water
Salt and freshly ground black pepper to taste

Method
Place the fish heads and water in a large pot and bring to the boil, then simmer covered for 30 minutes. Remove from the heat and strain. Pick the flesh from the fish heads and return to the stock. Add bananas and remaining ingredients, bring to the boil, then reduce heat and simmer until bananas are soft but not mushy. Remove whole pepper, add extra water if the soup is too thick, and serve hot.

Serves 4 to 5

Classic Caribbean Cooking

Green Pigeon Pea Soup

Puerto Rico

Ingredients
450 g/1 lb green pigeon peas
1.4 litres/2½ pints chicken stock or water
300 ml/10 fl oz sofrito (see page 294)
450 g/1 lb West Indian pumpkin, peeled and cubed
1 medium onion, chopped
Salt and freshly ground black pepper

Method
Place all the ingredients in a large pot, except the pumpkin, and cook for 30 minutes or until the peas are soft. Add pumpkin and continue to cook on a low heat until the pumpkin has disintegrated and thickened the soup. Season to taste, then serve hot.

Serves 7

Green Plantain Soup

Dominican Republic

Ingredients
1.4 litres/2½ pints beef stock
3 green plantains, peeled and sliced
1 medium onion, chopped
4 tablespoons cooking oil
Parmesan cheese, grated
Salt and freshly ground white pepper

Method
Pre-soak the plantains in cold water for 30 minutes and then dry with kitchen paper. Place the beef stock in a saucepan and heat. Sauté the sliced plantain until tender, about 5 to 10 minutes, then mash. Sauté the onion until translucent. Transfer the mashed plantain and sautéed onion to the stock, stir once and simmer for 15 minutes. Serve garnished with grated parmesan cheese.

Serves 5 to 6

Groundnut Soup

Nevis

Ingredients
240 ml/8 fl oz evaporated milk or single cream
1.2 litres/2 pints water or chicken stock
110 g/4 oz roasted groundnuts (peanuts)
Spring onion tops for garnish
Dash hot pepper sauce
Dash sherry (optional)
Salt and freshly ground black pepper

Method
Place the groundnuts and enough water to cover in a processor or blender, and blend to a smooth paste. Pour into a heavy saucepan and add remainder of the water or stock. Season, stir and simmer for 15 minutes, then add the milk or cream and simmer for a further 5 minutes. If using sherry, add at this stage and serve. Garnish with spring onion tops.

Serves 5 to 6

Gungo Pea Soup

Jamaica

Ingredients
1 ham bone or knuckle
450 g/1 lb shin of beef
230 g/8 oz salt beef
680 g/1½ lb gungo peas, soaked overnight
450 g/1 lb yellow yam, peeled and cubed
3 cocos, peeled and sliced (see Glossary)
2 onions, finely chopped
1 whole green scotch bonnet pepper
2 cloves garlic, crushed
2 sprigs thyme
230 g/8 oz plain flour (to make spinners)
2.3 litres/4 pints water
Freshly ground black pepper

Method
Drain the soaked peas and place in a large pot with the water, shin of beef, salt beef and ham bone. Boil for 10 minutes, then reduce the heat and cover. Cook for 2 hours or until the meat and peas are tender, then add the yam, cocos, thyme, onion, scotch bonnet pepper and garlic. Simmer for 15 minutes, then remove whole pepper, cut the meat from the bones and return to the soup. Add the spinners (see page 271) and cook for a further 15 minutes. Serve hot as a complete meal.

Serves 5 to 6

Classic Caribbean Cooking

Hot Banana Soup

St Lucia

Ingredients
14 green bananas
750 ml/1¼ pints lamb stock
110 g/4 oz grated coconut
½ hot pepper, de-seeded and finely chopped
2 spring onion stalks, finely chopped
1 measure white rum

Method
Sauté the grated coconut with the hot pepper in a dry frying pan for three minutes. Peel and chop bananas and place in a large saucepan with the stock. Cook for 25 minutes or until bananas are tender. Liquidise into a puree and return to the pan. Add the rum, spring onion, sautéed coconut and hot pepper. Heat through and serve with toast.

Serves 6

Jamaican Creole Soup

Jamaica

Ingredients
900 g/2 lb beef soup meat
450 g/1 lb pigs' tails
450 g/1 lb Jamaican red peas, soaked overnight
230 g/8 oz yam
1 whole green scotch bonnet pepper
4 spring onions, finely chopped
3 sprigs thyme
3 pimento (allspice) berries
450 g/1 lb flour (to make spinners)
2.3 litres/4 pints water

Method
Rinse the pre-soaked peas in cold water, then add to a large pot with the water and bring to the boil. After 10 minutes, skim and reduce heat, then add all the ingredients except the yam and flour. Simmer for 2 hours or until meat and peas are tender. Remove the pepper and discard. Remove the meat and chop into bite-size pieces. Liquidise the peas, add extra water at this stage if the soup is too thick. Return the meat to the pot. Add the spinners (see page 271) and diced yam and cook for another 15 minutes and serve.

Serves 6 to 8

Classic Caribbean Cooking

Lobster Soup

St Lucia

Ingredients

2 or 3 live lobsters
300 ml/10 fl oz single cream
2 shallots, chopped
1 clove garlic, peeled
2 tablespoons diced carrots
1 tablespoon chopped onion
3 sprigs parsley, finely chopped
1 sprig thyme
1 fresh bay leaf

1 pinch paprika
1 teaspoon tomato paste
1 glass dry white wine
½glass brandy
60 g/2 oz unsalted butter
300 ml/10 fl oz cold water
3 drops red food colouring (optional)
Salt and freshly ground black pepper

Method

Wash the lobsters under cold running water. Melt the butter in a large pot, then add onions, shallots, bay leaf, parsley, garlic and paprika, and cook for 5 minutes on a low heat. Add the live lobsters, cover and cook for 10 minutes or until the lobsters turn pink. Pour in the brandy and set it alight. When the flames subside, add salt and pepper and a glass of wine, and cover and cook for 10 minutes on a low heat. Remove lobsters and allow to cool, then remove all the lobster meat, place in a blender or processor with the water, and blend for 3 minutes. Pour mixture back into the pot, add food colouring (optional) or hot pepper sauce to taste. Serve hot.

Serves 6

Okra Soup

Jamaica

Ingredients
18 okra
450 g/1 lb salt beef
450 g/1 lb callaloo (or spinach), finely chopped
3 tomatoes, skinned and chopped
1 red scotch bonnet pepper, de-seeded and chopped
1 medium onion, finely chopped
2 sprigs thyme
750 ml/1¼ pints cold water
Freshly ground black pepper

Method
Pre-soak the salt beef in cold water for 1 hour. Top and tail the okra and slice into rings. Drain the beef then place in a large pot with the okra, tomatoes, pepper, thyme and onion, cover with water, and bring to the boil. Then cook on a low heat for about 2 hours or until beef is tender. Add the callaloo and cook for a further 20 minutes. Season to taste and serve.

Serves 4 to 5

Classic Caribbean Cooking

Onion Soup

Martinique

Ingredients
1.4 litres/2½ pints rich beef stock
1.8 kg/4 lb small onions
1 clove garlic, finely chopped
90 ml/3 fl oz brandy
60 g/2 oz grated gruyere cheese
4 tablespoons unsalted butter
½ teaspoon sugar
6 slices fried white bread

Method
Peel and slice the onions into thin rings. Heat the butter in a large pan and sauté the onions and garlic over a low heat for 10 minutes. Add the sugar and stir until the onions have caramelised. Heat brandy in a ladle over a flame or in a small saucepan and pour onto onions, then set alight. When flames subside, add stock and simmer for 1 hour. Pour into soup bowls and float croutons (fried bread cut into 1 inch squares) on top, and sprinkle with grated cheese. Serve hot.

Serves 6

Oxtail Soup

Bahamas

Ingredients

1.3 kg/3 lb lean oxtail, jointed
3 spring onions, finely chopped
3 medium carrots, sliced
1 whole hot pepper
1 small onion, finely chopped
1 clove garlic, chopped
2 sprigs thyme
6 pimento (allspice) berries
2 tablespoons dry sherry
230 g/8 oz flour (to make spinners)
Water

Method

Place jointed oxtail in a large soup kettle and cover with water. Boil for 10 minutes, then simmer for 30 minutes. Add carrots, pimento, spring onions, garlic, onion and thyme and continue to cook on a low heat until the meat is tender, about 2 hours. Leave to stand overnight, then remove the fat from the surface and bring back to the boil, adding more water if the soup is too thick. Add spinners (see page 271) then cook for 15 minutes and serve.

Serves 6 as a substantial soup

Oxtail Soup

Trinidad and Tobago

Ingredients
1.1 kg/2½ lb lean oxtail, chopped
110 g/4 oz lima beans, pre-soaked
3 medium carrots, peeled and sliced
2 large potatoes, peeled and cubed
1 small onion, finely chopped
3 spring onion stalks, chopped
1 whole hot pepper
1 clove garlic, chopped
2 sprigs thyme
30 g/1 oz salt

Method
Place oxtail, lima beans, onion and thyme in a large saucepan or soup kettle and cover with water. Bring to the boil then simmer for 2 to 3 hours. Remove from the heat and leave to stand overnight. Skim the fat from the surface, then heat the soup and add the carrots, garlic, potatoes, pepper, spring onions and salt, and cook for 20 minutes. Season to taste and remove pepper before serving.

Serving suggestion
This is a main course soup and only requires bread as an accompaniment.

Serves 6

Pepperpot Soup

Jamaica

Ingredients

680 g/1½ lb beef soup meat
450 g/1 lb pigs' tails
450 g/1 lb cooked shrimps
900 g/2 lb spinach or
callaloo, finely chopped
680 g/1½ lb kale, finely
chopped
230 g/8 oz coco, peeled
and chopped (see Glossary)
12 okras
3 spring onions, finely
chopped

1 small yellow garden egg
(a type of aubergine), diced
1 medium onion, finely
chopped
1 clove garlic, crushed
2 sprigs thyme
150 ml/5 fl oz coconut milk
2.3 litres/4 pints water
Salt and freshly ground
black pepper

Method

Place the beef soup meat and pigs' tails in a large pot with the water and bring to the boil. Simmer for 2 hours or until the meat is tender. Meanwhile, steam all the vegetables in a separate saucepan for 10 minutes, then liquidise to form a puree. Add the pureed vegetables and all the seasonings to the simmering meat approximately 15 minutes before the end of cooking time. Add more water if the mixture is too thick. Finally, stir in the coconut milk and cooked shrimps and simmer for a further 5 minutes. Serve hot.

Serves 6 to 8 as a main course soup

Author's note: This soup should not be confused with 'Pepperpot', the well-known dishes from Guyana and Antigua (See recipes in Pork).

Pumpkin Soup with Beef

St Lucia

Ingredients
1.1 kg/2½ lb brisket or stewing beef
900 g/2 lb pumpkin, peeled, de-seeded and diced
2 carrots, peeled and finely chopped
1½ medium onions, chopped
1 spring onion, finely chopped
1 potato, quartered
½ green capsicum, de-seeded
3 cloves garlic, crushed
2 sprigs thyme
2 teaspoons hot curry powder
1 tablespoon tomato paste
2.3 litres/4 pints cold water

Method
Place meat, water and pumpkin in a large pot or soup kettle, bring to the boil then simmer for 1½ to 2 hours, or until meat is tender. Add all the remaining ingredients, except the potato, top up with more water to cover the vegetables and cook for a further 30 minutes. Add salt and potato and cook for a further 15 minutes to thicken ensuring that the vegetables are cooked. Serve hot.

Serves 6

202

Sweet Potato Soup

Grenada

Ingredients
450 g/1 lb sweet potatoes, peeled and diced
1 medium onion, chopped
3 stalks celery, chopped
1.2 litres/2 pints chicken stock or water
150 ml/5 fl oz single cream
Pinch freshly grated nutmeg
1 tablespoon cooking oil
½ teaspoon freshly ground black pepper
½ teaspoon salt

Method
Sauté the sweet potato, onion and celery in a saucepan for 5 minutes. Add stock and simmer for 20 minutes, or until potato is soft, then liquidise. Return to the saucepan and add single cream. Stir and season with salt, pepper and nutmeg, and serve.

Serves 5 to 6

Tannia Soup

Dominica

Ingredients
900 g/2 lb tannia, peeled and chopped
450 g/1 lb salt pork, cubed
1.4 litres/2½ pints water or chicken stock
170 g/6 oz chopped tomatoes
1 onion, finely chopped
1 sprig thyme
3 tablespoons unsalted butter
Freshly ground black pepper

Method
Melt the butter in a large soup kettle or pot and sauté the pork and onions, taking care that the onions do not caramelise. Add the stock, tannias, tomatoes, thyme and pepper and cook over a low heat for about 25 minutes so that the tannias become tender, not mushy. Serve hot.

Serves 5 to 6

Tripe Soup

Curaçao

Ingredients

900 g/2 lb tripe
2 pig's trotters, split and cleaned
230 g/8 oz salt beef
450 g/1 lb West Indian pumpkin, peeled and cubed
3 potatoes, peeled and cubed
1 sweet potato, peeled and cubed
1 green capsicum, de-seeded and thinly sliced
1 stalk celery, chopped
60 g/2 oz chopped spring onions
5 pitted green olives
60 ml/2 fl oz freshly squeezed lime juice
1 tablespoon raisins
½ tablespoon capers
½ teaspoon ground cloves
½ teaspoon freshly grated nutmeg
2.3 litres/4 pints water

Method

Wash and drain the tripe, then pour lime juice over and marinate for 15 minutes. Place the trotters and tripe in a large pot with the water, bring to the boil, then simmer for 3 hours, or until meat is tender. Meanwhile, soak beef in boiling water for 1 hour then add to the trotters and tripe mid-way through cooking time. When cooked, remove the meat, tripe and trotters from the pot and allow cool. Cut the tripe into 2.5 cm/1 inch strips, cut the beef into 1 inch cubes, de-bone the trotters and return all to the soup. Add the remaining ingredients and simmer for 30 minutes or until vegetables are tender. Leave to stand for 4 hours, to enhance the flavour, reheat and serve hot.

Serving suggestion

Serve as a main course

Serves 12 to 14

Classic Caribbean Cooking

Vegetable Soup

Jamaica

Ingredients
1 christophene (cho-cho)
230 g/8 oz West Indian pumpkin
230 g/8 oz yellow yam
230 g/8 oz okra
230 g/8 oz sweet potatoes
230 g/8 oz tomatoes, skinned and chopped
230 g/8 oz potatoes
230 g/8 oz carrots
1 medium onion, finely chopped
1 whole green scotch bonnet pepper
300 ml/10 fl oz coconut milk
3 cloves garlic, crushed
3 pimento (allspice) berries
2 sprigs thyme
450 g/1 lb flour (to make spinners)
1 litre/1¾ pints water
Salt and freshly ground black pepper

Method
Peel all the vegetables and chop into ½ inch pieces, then add to a large pot of salted boiling water. Add the garlic, pimento, thyme, whole scotch bonnet pepper and onion, and simmer for 20 minutes or until all vegetables are tender. Then add the spinners (see page 271) and cook for a further 15 minutes, stirring in the coconut milk for the last 5 minutes of cooking time. Serve hot as a main course soup.

Serves 5 to 6

Classic Caribbean Cooking

Vegetarian Ackee Soup

Jamaica

Ingredients
600 ml/1 pint vegetable stock
2 tins ackee
110 g/4 oz tomatoes, skinned and chopped
3 spring onions, chopped
1 slice scotch bonnet pepper, de-seeded
2 teaspoons curry powder
150 ml/5 fl oz double cream (optional)
Salt and freshly ground black pepper

Method
Place all the ingredients in a large saucepan except the double cream (if using) and simmer for 10 minutes or until the tomatoes and spring onions are soft. Season to taste then liquidise. Add double cream (if using), reheat or chill and serve.

Serves 5 to 6

Dessert

Baked Pineapple

Barbados

Ingredients
1 medium pineapple
60 g/2 oz Demerara sugar
4 tablespoons rum
2 teaspoons powdered cinnamon
2 teaspoons desiccated coconut

Method
Prepare pineapple by cutting lengthways and then scooping out flesh without piercing the shell. Discard hard core and pith, dice flesh and retain the juice. Coat the pineapple shell in a mixture of sugar and 2 tablespoons of rum. Return the flesh to the shell, pour over juice and bake at gas mark 4, 375°F, 180°C, for 20 minutes or until tender. Heat remainder of the rum and pour over the baked pineapple, set alight and serve flaming. Eat when flames subside.

Serving suggestion
Sprinkle coconut on baked pineapple and serve with ice cream or sorbet.

Serves 4 to 6

Banana Delight

St Lucia

Ingredients
6 large ripe bananas
6 tablespoons dark rum
60 g/2 oz grated coconut
Juice of 1 freshly squeezed lime

Method
Peel and split the bananas lengthways and place in a buttered oven-proof dish. Sprinkle with sugar and pour lime juice over bananas. Cook in a preheated oven at gas mark 4, 350°F, 180°C, for 20 minutes. Cover with grated coconut and rum.

Serving suggestion
Serve hot with whipped cream or vanilla or banana ice cream

Serves 6

Banana Nut Pudding

Tobago

Ingredients
4 bananas, sliced
450 ml/15 fl oz milk
4 slices 1 cm/½ inch thick bread, buttered
110 g/4 oz chopped cashew nuts
60 g/2 oz caster sugar
2 eggs, size 2
3 teaspoons grated lime rind
Grated nutmeg

Method
Remove the crusts and dice the bread, then butter a shallow oven-proof dish and place a layer of bread in the bottom. Sprinkle with half the nuts, then the sliced bananas. Add 30 g/1 oz of sugar and the lime rind, then the remainder of the nuts and the bread. Beat the eggs with sugar, stir in the milk and pour over the pudding. Bake at gas mark 4, 350°F, 180°C, for 30 minutes or until it sets. Serve warm with Chantilly cream.

Serves 4

Banana Pudding

Martinique

Ingredients
6 large bananas, halved and split lengthways
300 ml/10 fl oz sweet red wine
300 ml/10 fl oz sugar syrup
4 tablespoons unsalted butter
½ teaspoon ground cinnamon

Method
Place the sugar syrup, wine and cinnamon in a saucepan and stir while heating to mix ingredients. Heat the butter in a flame-proof serving dish and sauté the bananas until brown on both sides. Pour wine mixture over the bananas and heat for 15 minutes on a low flame. Serve hot with whipped cream.

Serves 6

Banana Snow

Dominica

Ingredients
2 bananas, peeled and mashed
170 g/6 oz caster sugar
60 ml/2 fl oz freshly squeezed lemon or lime juice
2 egg whites, size 2
1 tablespoon gelatine
1 teaspoon grated lemon rind
60 ml/2 fl oz cold water
¼ teaspoon salt

Method
Place water in a double boiler with juice and the gelatine. Heat to soften and dissolve the gelatine, making sure it does not boil. Allow to cool, then pour into a large bowl and leave until partially set. Pour in the bananas and smooth out. Whisk the egg whites with the salt until stiff. Then fold in the sugar - 30 g/1 oz at a time - with a metal spoon. Pour into the bowl and leave in the refrigerator for at least 3 hours until firm.

Serves 2 –3

Bojo

Surinam

Ingredients
1.1 g/2½ lb sweet cassava, finely grated
340 g/12 oz desiccated coconut
300 ml/10 fl oz full cream milk
110 g/4 oz light brown sugar
80 g/3 oz unsalted butter, melted
80 g/3 oz raisins
1 teaspoon vanilla essence
½ teaspoon almond essence
½ teaspoon ground cinnamon
¼ teaspoon nutmeg, freshly grated

Method
Beat the sugar, vanilla and almond in a large oven-proof bowl. Heat milk and butter together, then add this and remaining ingredients to the bowl and stir. Pour into a non-stick, 9-inch cake tin and bake in a pre-heated oven at gas mark 5, 375°F, 190°C, for 1½ hours, or until golden. Serve warm.

Serves 5 to 6

Candied Peel

Jamaica

Ingredients
230 g/8 oz orange peel
280 g/10 oz granulated sugar
1 tablespoon golden syrup
300 ml/10 fl oz cold water

Method
Remove the peel from the fruit and scrape away all the pith. This is more easily done once the peel has been boiled. Put the peel in water and bring to the boil, reduce the heat, cover, and simmer for 10 minutes. Drain and repeat twice. When cooked leave to cool and then cut peel into ½ inch strips. Put 230 g/8 oz of granulated sugar in a clean pan with 300 ml/10 fl oz of cold water and the golden syrup. Bring to the boil, stirring constantly, then simmer for 30 minutes. The liquid should have been absorbed and the peel should be moist and sticky, not dry. Drain on kitchen paper for 15 minutes, and then sprinkle with the remainder of the granulated sugar. Leave to dry uncovered for 2 days, then store in a preserving jar, until ready for use. They will keep for up to 3 weeks.

Author's note: This process can be used for limes, lemons, tangerines and grapefruit.

Cassava Pone

Guyana

Ingredients
2 medium cassavas
1 small ripe coconut
170 g/6 oz sugar
60 g/2 oz butter
1 teaspoon mixed spice
1 teaspoon vanilla essence
1 teaspoon freshly ground black pepper
1 teaspoon salt

Method
Grate the cassava and coconut and work in the softened butter with a fork. Add sugar, spice, essence and a little milk to bind the mixture. Add pepper and salt and turn into a greased baking dish. The pone should be about an inch thick. Bake in a moderate oven at gas mark 4, 350°F, 180°C, for 30 minutes or until the top is crisp and brown.

Serves 4 to 5

Cassava Pudding

Jamaica

Ingredients
340 g/12 oz sweet cassava flour
340 g/12 oz coconut cream
250 g/9 oz brown sugar
110 g/4 oz grated coconut
80 g/3 oz wholemeal flour
60 g/2 oz unsalted butter
2 eggs, size 2
1 teaspoon vanilla essence
Rind of half a small orange
½ teaspoon salt

Method
Mix all the dry ingredients together. Add melted butter, coconut cream, beaten eggs and vanilla. Beat well. Pour mixture into a greased shallow oven-proof baking dish and bake in a moderate oven at gas mark 3, 325°F, 160°C, for 1½ hours or until knife comes out cleanly when inserted into top of pudding.

Serves 6

Chantilly Cream

Martinique

Ingredients
600 ml/1 pint double cream
4 teaspoons sugar
3 teaspoons vanilla essence

Method
Pour the cream into a bowl, add the sugar and vanilla essence and beat until the mixture forms stiff peaks.

Serving suggestion
Serve with fruitcakes or as a topping for any sweet dish.

Chocolate Cream Pudding

Guyana

Ingredients
750 ml/1¼ pints milk
110 g/4 oz Demerara sugar
80 g/3 oz unsweetened cocoa
30 g/1 oz cornflour
2 teaspoons vanilla essence

Method
Sift the cornflour with the cocoa and sugar and place in a saucepan. Gradually stir in the milk over a low heat until free of lumps. Mixture should be thick enough to coat the back of a wooden spoon. Add vanilla when slightly cooled, pour into a serving dish and refrigerate until required. Serve chilled.

Serves 6

Citrus and Rum Sorbet

Martinique

Ingredients
300 ml/10 fl oz freshly squeezed orange juice
3 tablespoons caster sugar
2 tablespoons white rum
1 tablespoon freshly squeezed lime juice
½ tablespoon freshly grated lime rind
1½ teaspoons powdered gelatine
8 strips candied orange and lime peel (see page 214)
150 ml/5 fl oz cold water

Method
Sprinkle the gelatine over 2 tablespoons of water in a double boiler, or a small heat-proof bowl. Leave until spongy, and then stand over simmering water, making sure that the bowl does not touch the water. Heat slowly until the gelatine has dissolved, remove from heat. In a heavy-based saucepan, bring the remainder of the water and sugar to the boil and stir until sugar has dissolved, then simmer for 1 minute. Stir in the gelatine and then add fruit juices, rum and lime rind. Cook for 30 seconds on a low heat. Remove from heat and cool. At this stage, if you have an electric ice-cream maker follow manufacturer's instructions. If not, strain into a shallow freezer-proof container and freeze until slushy, about 1 hour. Tip into a bowl and beat until smooth then freeze until solid. Chill some stem dishes or glasses and serve decorated with strips of candied peel.

Serves 4

Coffee and Rum Sauce

Jamaica

Ingredients
120 ml/4 fl oz hot, strong black coffee
75 ml/2½ fl oz double cream
2 large egg yolks
2 tablespoons dark rum
1 tablespoon milk
1 teaspoon cornflour

Method
Place coffee in the top half of a double boiler or a saucepan set over a pan of simmering water ensuring that the bottom of the bowl does not touch the water. Add sugar and dissolve, then add egg yolks one at a time and combine thoroughly after each addition. Stir in cream and cook for 1 to 2 minutes then allow to cool. Mix together the milk and cornflour then add to the saucepan. Heat gently and stir constantly until sauce thickens, finally add the rum.

Serving suggestion
This sauce can be served hot with ice cream or meringues, or cold with fruit salad.

Makes 240 ml/8 fl oz

Classic Caribbean Cooking

Coffee Crush

Jamaica

Ingredients
600 ml/1 pint strong Blue Mountain Coffee
3 tablespoons Tia Maria or similar liqueur
4 chocolate coated coffee beans
Whipped cream

Method
Sweeten coffee with three tablespoons of sugar then allow to cool. When cold, pour into ice cube trays and freeze. Remove from freezer 5 to 10 minutes before serving and crush the ice cubes (in an automatic crusher or similar) until mixture is slushy. Spoon into well chilled sundae dishes. Pour Tia Maria over the crushed ice, add whipped cream and top each one with a chocolate coffee bean and serve.

Serves 4

Coffee Sauce

Jamaica

Ingredients
300 ml/10 fl oz strong black coffee
2 heaped tablespoons soft brown sugar
2 level tablespoons arrowroot ·
30 g/1 oz unsalted butter

Method
Mix the arrowroot with a small amount of cold water to the consistency of custard. Heat the coffee and sugar in a small saucepan. Once sugar has dissolved, add the arrowroot. When the sauce has thickened, beat in the butter.

Serving suggestion
Serve with ice cream or any chocolate, pineapple or coffee dessert.

Serves 6

Cornmeal Pone

Trinidad and Tobago

Ingredients
170 g/6 oz cornmeal
230 g/8 oz finely grated coconut
230 g/8 oz pumpkin, peeled, grated
60 g/2 oz seedless raisins
60 g/2 oz sugar
60 g/2 oz unsalted butter, melted
1 teaspoon ground allspice
½ teaspoon salt

Method
Mix together coconut, raisins, salt, grated pumpkin, sugar, cornmeal and allspice and stir in the butter. Add enough milk to make a stiff batter and whisk for 2 minutes. Pour into a shallow oven-proof baking dish and bake at gas mark 4, 350°F, 180°C, for 30 minutes or until a knife comes out clean when inserted in the top of the pudding. Serve warm.

Serves 6

Flamed Shaddock

Jamaica

Ingredients
2 shaddock (see Glossary)
60 g/2 oz unsalted butter
6 tablespoons Appleton white rum
4 tablespoons brown sugar

Method
Peel and cut the shaddock into segments making sure that all the pith is removed. Heat the shaddock segments in melted butter and sugar in a large frying pan for 3 minutes. Take care not to burn the butter. Warm the rum then pour over and ignite. Serve when the flames subside.

Serving suggestion
Serve on its own or use as a filling for a sweet crêpe or with an orange sorbet.

Serves 4

Floating Islands

Barbados

Ingredients
450 g/15 fl oz single cream
6 tablespoons double cream
60 g/2 oz caster sugar
3 eggs, size 2, separated
3 tablespoons Cockspur Rum
3 tablespoons guava jelly
1 tablespoon sugar
1 teaspoon vanilla

Method
Combine the egg yolks and sugar and whisk until the egg yolks are light and pale in colour. Heat the single cream to boiling point and pour into egg mixture. Place in the top of a double boiler. The mixture should be stirred constantly over a low heat until it can coat the back of a wooden spoon. Do not boil. When thick, stir in the vanilla essence, pour into a serving dish and refrigerate. Next, soften the guava jelly by beating with a fork. Whisk the egg whites until stiff, fold in the guava jelly and drop teaspoons onto the chilled custard. Whip cream with 1 tablespoon of sugar and the rum and serve chilled, separately.

Serves 6

Frozen Egg Nog

Jamaica

Ingredients
300 ml/10 fl oz double or whipping cream
3 tablespoons caster sugar
2 egg yolks, size 2
2 tablespoons Appleton Rum, dark or golden
1 tablespoon brandy
4 slices pineapple or mango to decorate

Method
Place egg yolks, sugar, rum and brandy in a double boiler or in a pan over hot water and whisk until the mixture is thick and creamy. Remove from the heat and continue whisking until the mixture has cooled slightly. Transfer to a freezer-proof container. Whip the cream until it stands in soft peaks, and then fold carefully into the egg mixture. Freeze for a minimum of 4 hours. Serve in chilled bowls decorated with a slice of mango or pineapple.

Serves 4

Fruit Salad in Grenadine Syrup

The Grenadines

Ingredients
2 large paw-paw (papaya), peeled and de-seeded
1 large mango, peeled and stoned
2 sweet oranges, peeled and chopped
3 passion fruit, pulp removed from shell
½ melon, peeled, de-seeded and cubed
4 tablespoons freshly squeezed lime juice, strained
3 tablespoons grenadine
5 cm/2 inches fresh ginger root
60 g/2 oz sugar
1 litre/1¾ pints water

Method
Place all the fruit in a large bowl, toss with lime juice and refrigerate for 1 hour. Place the peeled and sliced ginger in a large saucepan, cover with water and add the sugar. Bring to the boil, then reduce heat and simmer until the sugar has dissolved and the syrup has reduced by half. Cool for 20 minutes then remove the ginger and stir in the grenadine. Pour syrup over the chilled fruit and return to the refrigerator for 1½ hours.

Serves 8 as a first course or 6 as a dessert.

Ginger Cream

Trinidad

Ingredients
150 ml/5 fl oz whipped cream
150 ml/5 fl oz milk
60 g/2 oz preserved chopped ginger
2 eggs, size 2
4 tablespoons rum
2 tablespoons caster sugar
1 heaped teaspoon gelatine
1 tablespoon water

Method
Separate the eggs and stir the sugar into the egg yolks. Place the yolks and the milk in the top of a double boiler and stir constantly until the mixture is thick. Do not boil. Dissolve the gelatine in 1 tablespoon of water. Cool slightly then fold in the whipped cream, ginger and stiffly beaten egg whites. Pour into a prepared mould and chill until set.

Serves 3 to 4

Grapefruit Fritters

British Virgin Islands

Ingredients
2 large grapefruits, peeled, cut into rings with pith removed
110 g/4 oz plain flour
30 g/1 oz caster sugar
Milk
Oil for deep frying
Icing sugar for dusting

Method
Start by making the batter. Sift the flour, add sugar and stir in enough milk until you have a fairly stiff batter. Leave to stand for 1½ hours. Next, heat the oil to smoking point, dip the grapefruit rings into the batter and fry one at a time. Fry quickly until golden brown, then drain on kitchen paper and serve dusted with icing sugar.

Serving suggestion
For a more luxurious dessert you can serve with a fruit sorbet and a fruit sauce

Serves 4

Green Banana Pudding

St Lucia

Ingredients
1 large green banana
300 ml/10 fl oz milk
2 eggs, size 2
2 tablespoons sugar
1 teaspoon vanilla essence
¼ teaspoon freshly grated nutmeg

Method
Peel banana and grate on a fine grater, combine with 2 tablespoons of milk. Add sugar to remaining milk and add vanilla, nutmeg and beaten eggs. Mix well. Pour into an oven-proof dish and bake at gas mark 4, 350°F, 180°C, for 30 minutes or until brown. Serve hot or cold.

Serves 2

Latter-day Saints

Trinidad

Ingredients
2 grapefruits
Pulp of 2 oranges
60 g/2 oz brown sugar
30 g/1 oz unsalted butter

Method
Cut the grapefruits in half and remove flesh, at the same time discarding the pith. Mix grapefruit flesh with the orange pulp and return to the grapefruit shells. Top each half with butter and brown sugar and slow grill for about 5 minutes or until the fruit is hot and the sugar and butter have melted. Serve hot.

Serves 4

Lime Ice Cream

Martinique

Ingredients
12 limes
340g/12 oz caster sugar
300 ml/10 fl oz double cream
Grated zest of 3 limes
300 ml/10 fl oz water

Method
Squeeze the limes then add the juice to the water and sugar.
Bring to the boil, then simmer for 3 minutes. Add the grated
zest, then boil rapidly for 2 minutes. Cool then add whipped
cream. Freeze for 4 to 6 hours or place in the bowl of an ice
cream machine and follow instructions. Serve with a slice of
fresh lime on top.

Serves 4

Mango Fool

Guyana

Ingredients
340 g/12 oz mango puree
600 ml/1 pint stiffly whipped double cream
110 g/4 oz Demerara sugar
1 tablespoon lime juice

Method
Mix the sugar and lime into the puree. Chill thoroughly. Just before serving blend the cream into the puree. A tablespoon of rum may be added at this point.

Serves 4

Melon Ice

Grenada

Ingredients
900g/2 lb very ripe water melon flesh, seeds removed
110g/4 oz caster sugar
Juice of 1 medium lime
150 ml/5 fl oz water

Method
Puree the watermelon flesh. Place the sugar and water in a pan
and heat gently until sugar has dissolved. Boil rapidly for 4
minutes, and then pour into a bowl, allow to cool then chill
in the refrigerator. When chilled, mix in lime juice and melon
and freeze for at least 3 hours. Beat the mixture after 1 hour to
remove ice crystals.

Serving suggestion
Serve with a slice of watermelon on the side and thin crisp biscuits.

Serves 4

Orange Sorbet

Curaçao

Ingredients
180 ml/6 fl oz freshly squeezed orange juice
170g/6 oz sugar
2 egg whites, size 2
2 tablespoons curaçao (see Glossary)
450g/15 fl oz water

Method
Place the sugar and water in a pan, heating gently and stirring constantly until the sugar has dissolved. Boil for 5 minutes. Place the orange juice in a bowl, cool the syrup then combine with juice and freeze in a shallow dish for 2 hours until thick and slushy. Beat the egg whites until stiff peaks can be formed. Fold into the mixture with a metal spoon and return container to freezer for at least 2 hours before serving. Serve in chilled dishes decorated with slices of fresh orange and with the curaçao drizzled over the top.

Serves 4

Passion Fruit Ice Cream

Dominica

Ingredients
6 passion fruits
300 ml/10 fl oz double cream
2 egg yolks, size 2
Liquid sweetener to taste
2 passion fruits for topping

Method
Halve the 6 passion fruits, scoop out the pulp and place in a large bowl with liquid sweetener, cream and egg yolks. Mix well together, then pour into a shallow rigid container and freeze. After 1 hour, remove from freezer, break down ice crystals with a fork and then return to freezer. Leave until set, about 3 hours, and then remove at least 10 minutes before serving. Serve in chilled dishes and top with passion fruit pulp made from the remaining two passion fruits.

Serves 4

Pekin Dust

Aruba

Ingredients
680 g/1½ lb chestnuts, fresh or vacuum-packed
6 tablespoons double cream, beaten thick
110 g/4 oz caster sugar
1 teaspoon powdered ginger
¼ teaspoon salt
Slices peeled orange
Chopped nuts

Method
Place chestnuts, which have been slit on top, but are still in the shells, in a large saucepan of salted water (vacuum-packed chestnuts are already skinned, so follow the instructions). Boil until the chestnuts are tender and the shells burst, then drain and peel. Allow to cool then puree in a food processor until a paste is formed. Stir in the ginger, sugar and cream. Place the mixture in a greased mould and leave in a refrigerator for 1 hour. Turn out and decorate with a sprinkling of chopped nuts and sliced oranges.

Serves 6 to 8

Pina Colada Sorbet

Puerto Rico

Ingredients
450 ml/15 fl oz freshly squeezed pineapple juice
4 tablespoons caster sugar
3 tablespoons freshly squeezed lime juice
2 tablespoons coconut milk powder
4 teaspoons grated lime rind
2 egg whites, size 2
Slices of pineapple and passion fruit pulp
300 ml/10 fl oz cold water

Method
Place the water, juices and lime rind in a heavy base saucepan and stir in the sugar and heat gently until the sugar has dissolved. Increase heat and boil rapidly until the thread stage is reached (225°F on a sugar thermometer). Remove from heat and immediately add the coconut milk powder. Leave to cool. If freezing without the benefit of a machine, you will have to whip the egg whites until they form soft peaks, then fold into semi-frozen pineapple mixture that has been frozen for 1½ hours, then beat at hourly intervals for the next three hours. If using a machine combine all the ingredients and follow instructions. Serve with a thin slice of pineapple and the pulp of one passion fruit spooned over the top.

Serves 4

Pineapple and Ginger Treat

Jamaica

Ingredients
½ fresh pineapple, cored and cubed
110 g/4 oz water melon, de-seeded and diced
2 bananas
150 ml/5 fl oz whipped double cream
150 g/5 fl oz sugar syrup
2 tablespoons ginger syrup
2 tablespoons preserved ginger, finely chopped
2 tablespoons freshly squeezed and strained lime juice

Method
Peel and slice bananas and toss in lime juice. Add ginger, melon and pineapple cubes, together with both syrups. Place in a glass dish and chill for at least 3 hours to allow flavours to blend. Serve in individual dishes topped with whipped cream.

Serves 4

Pineapple Mousse

Martinique

Ingredients
450 g/15 fl oz freshly squeezed pineapple juice
230 g/8 oz caster sugar
6 egg whites, size 2
1 tablespoon arrowroot
Pinch salt

Method
Beat the egg whites with the salt until stiff. Pour the pineapple juice into a saucepan but reserve a small amount to mix with the arrowroot to form a thin paste. Add sugar to juice and stir over a moderate heat until dissolved. Add arrowroot to mixture and continue stirring until slightly thickened. Cool, then fold egg whites into pineapple mixture with a metal spoon. Turn into a glass serving dish and refrigerate for 3 to 4 hours before serving. Can be served with whipped Chantilly cream (see page 217).

Serve 6

Pitch Lake Pudding

Trinidad

Ingredients
300 ml/10 fl oz double cream
230 g/8 oz caster sugar
110 g/4 oz unsweetened cocoa
5 eggs, size 2, separated
6 tablespoons Trinidadian rum
2 tablespoons coffee essence

Method
Whisk the egg whites with the salt until they form soft peaks. Dissolve the cocoa in a large basin over hot water, add the coffee essence and the sugar then whisk for 5 minutes until sugar has dissolved. Add the egg yolks and whisk over the heat until they have doubled in volume, then add the rum. Pour cocoa mixture carefully into egg yolks and combine with a metal spoon. Finally, fold in the egg whites and pour mixture into a large glass bowl. Refrigerate overnight. Serve with whipped cream.

Serves 6

Pumpkin and Coconut Pudding

Dominica

Ingredients
450 g/1 lb uncooked pumpkin
450 g/1 lb sweet potatoes
1 medium coconut
600 ml/1 pint evaporated milk
230 g/8 oz brown sugar
230 g/8 oz unsalted butter
6 eggs, size 2

Method
Peel and grate pumpkin, coconut and potato and place in a large bowl. In another bowl cream together sugar and butter until light and fluffy and add to grated ingredients. Mix thoroughly. Add beaten eggs and milk to mixture, then pour into a buttered oven-proof dish and bake for about 40 minutes at gas mark 4, 350°F, 180°C, or until a knife comes out cleanly. Serve hot or cold.

Serves 6 to 8

Raisin Sauce

Barbados

Ingredients
140 ml/5 oz seedless raisins
1 lemon
60 g/2 oz caster sugar
30 g/1 oz unsalted butter
2 tablespoons treacle
1 teaspoon cornflour
Grated rind of lemon
300 ml/10 fl oz water

Method
Place raisins in enough water to cover and leave to soak for 1 hour. Mix treacle, sugar, lemon juice and the mixed cornflour with the raisin water in a saucepan. Bring to the boil then simmer for 10 minutes. Stir in the raisins, lemon rind and butter, and serve hot over bananas or pineapple.

Rum and Raisin Ice Cream

Guyana

Ingredients
300 ml/10 fl oz double cream, whipped
110 g/4 oz icing sugar, sifted
110 g/4 oz seedless raisins
4 tablespoons dark or golden rum
4 eggs, size 2, separated

Method
Put the rum and raisins in a bowl and leave to marinate overnight. The following day, put egg yolks and sugar in a bowl and whisk together until pale and fluffy, then fold in the whipped cream with a metal spoon. Stir in the marinated raisins then stiffly beat the egg whites and fold carefully into the rest of the mixture with a metal spoon. Pour into a rigid freezer-proof container and freeze for at least 3 hours. Remove from the freezer 10 minutes before eating. Decorate with more raisins and a drizzle of rum if preferred.

Serves 6 to 8

Rum Omelette

Jamaica

Ingredients
4 eggs, size 2
Guava jelly or Seville orange marmalade
1 tablespoon dark Jamaican rum
Unsalted butter

Method
Allow 1 egg per person. Separate the eggs and whisk the egg whites until stiff, then add 1 tablespoon of cold water to the yolks and stir. Melt butter in an omelette pan. Combine eggs and add to pan, fry until the underside is golden and the top well set, about 2 minutes on a medium to high heat. Avoid breaking when cooked. Carefully slide onto a serving plate and spread with jelly or marmalade and roll up quickly. In a ladle or small pan heat the rum, ignite and pour over the omelette immediately, and serve.

Serves 4

Seville Orange Custard

Cayman Islands

Ingredients
600 ml/1 pint hot milk
110 g/4 oz caster sugar
4 egg yolks, size 2
Juice of 1 Seville orange
Rind of ½ Seville orange
1 tablespoon brandy
Brown sugar for decoration

Method
Boil orange rind in 5 fl oz water until tender and then chop finely. Place the rind in a bowl, combine with juice, sugar, brandy and unbeaten egg yolks. Add the hot milk and mix well. Pour into ramekin dishes and place in a baking dish with about ½ inch of hot water. Bake covered loosely with foil at gas mark 3, 325°F, 160°C, for about 25 minutes. The dessert is ready when a knife inserted into the top comes out cleanly. Allow to cool. Before serving put a teaspoon of brown sugar over each ramekin and place under a very hot grill for around 2 minutes or until sugar caramelises.

Serves 4

Sweet Potato Pudding

Dominica

Ingredients
2 large sweet potatoes
600 ml/1 pint evaporated milk
2 eggs, size 2
1 piece of fresh ginger, about 1 inch long
2 teaspoons vanilla essence
1 teaspoon mixed spice
Sugar to taste

Method
Grate potato and ginger. Beat together milk and eggs to make custard. Pour milk onto grated potato and ginger. Stir well. Add flavourings and sugar to taste. Place in a buttered oven-proof dish. Bake at gas mark 3, 325°F, 160°C, for about 30 minutes or until knife comes out clean. Allow to cool, then cut into squares and serve.

Serves 6 to 8

Willemstad Oranges

Curaçao

Ingredients
6 large oranges
170 g/6 oz caster sugar
3 tablespoons curaçao

Method
Retain the peel from one orange and slice into fine strips, then place in cold water and leave for 30 minutes. Then boil in fresh water for 5 minutes to remove bitterness, drain and set aside. Peel the remaining oranges, remove pith and separate each segment, taking care to leave pith, skin and membrane behind. Lay segments in circles on a deep platter, sprinkle with curaçao and sugar and chill overnight.

Serving suggestion
Serve garnished with orange peel strips and orange sorbet.

Serves 6

Pastry,
Pies &
Biscuits

Banana Biscuits

St Lucia

Ingredients
2 very ripe bananas
140 g/5 oz plain flour
2 tablespoons sugar
1 tablespoon unsalted butter
2 teaspoons baking powder
¼ teaspoon salt

Method
Sift together the flour, salt and baking powder. Puree the bananas, then cream the butter and sugar together and combine all the ingredients to create a dough. If the mixture is too wet, add more flour. Place dough onto a floured surface, roll out and then cut out biscuit shapes with a pastry cutter. Place on a greased baking sheet and bake at gas mark 4, 350°F, 180°C, for 10 to 15 minutes or until brown.

Serving suggestion
Eat with banana ice cream, or on their own.

Makes about 10 to 12

Banana Tart

Grenada

Ingredients
8 ripe bananas
230 g/8 oz sweet shortcrust pastry
5 tablespoons sugar
60 g/2 oz unsalted butter
2 tablespoons dark rum
Juice of 1 freshly squeezed lime
120 ml/4 fl oz water

Method
Roll out pastry and line a 9-inch pie dish. Leave to rest for 30 minutes in a refrigerator. Peel 2 bananas, chop into small pieces and place in a heavy based saucepan with sugar, butter and rum. Bring to the boil then simmer until mixture thickens, then remove from the heat. Place the remaining peeled and sliced bananas in overlapping circles in the pastry shell. Sprinkle lime juice over, then pour in the cooked bananas. Bake in a preheated oven at gas mark 6, 400°F, 200°C, for 40 minutes or until browned.

Serves 6 to 8

Cho-Cho
(Christophene) Pie

Jamaica

Ingredients
4 cho-chos (christophenes)
450 g/1 lb sweet shortcrust pastry
230 g/8 oz caster sugar
Juice of 2 freshly squeezed limes
Grated rind of 1 lime
6 cloves
300 ml/10 fl oz cold water

Method
Peel, chop and core the cho-chos, then cut into bite-size pieces. Simmer in a saucepan on a medium heat with cloves and water until soft, this should take about 15 to 20 minutes. Cool and remove the cloves. Add sugar and lime juice to the water then boil rapidly to create thick syrup. Allow to cool. Line a pie dish with half the pastry. Place the cho-chos into the pastry, then pour in the cooled syrup. Sprinkle with the lime rind. Place a pie funnel in the middle of the dish then cover with the remaining pastry. Seal the edges with water, crimp and bake in a preheated oven at gas mark 6, 400°F, 200°C, for 40 minutes or until browned.

Serves 4 to 6

Fresh Coconut Cream Pie

St Vincent

Ingredients
230 g/8 oz freshly grated coconut
1 baked pie shell, 23 cm/9 inch
300 ml/10 fl oz double cream
750 ml/1¼ pints hot milk
170 g/6 oz granulated sugar
3 egg yolks, size 2, beaten
80 g/3 oz arrowroot
1 teaspoon vanilla essence
½ teaspoon almond essence
½ teaspoon salt

Method
Place sugar, arrowroot, salt and milk in a saucepan, gradually bring to the boil, stirring over a medium heat for 2 minutes. With the beaten egg yolks in a bowl, stir in some of the hot mixture, then pour the contents of the bowl into the saucepan and combine. Cook, stirring constantly, over a low heat for 5 minutes until the mixture is thick. Turn into a bowl, stir in the vanilla and almond essences and half the coconut. Lay waxed paper on the mixture to prevent a skin forming, and refrigerate for 3 hours. Then place mixture in the pie shell. Whip cream and fold in the remainder of the coconut, place on top of the pie and refrigerate for another 3 hours. Serve cold.

Serves 6 to 8

Lime Pie

Montserrat

Ingredients
300 ml/10 fl oz strained fresh lime juice
3 tablespoons freshly grated lime peel
25 cm/10 inch baked pie shell
230 g/8 oz caster sugar
2 eggs, size 2, well beaten
20 g/¾oz unsalted butter
2 tablespoons arrowroot
450 ml/15 fl oz water

Method
Mix the arrowroot with a little water to create a paste, then add to the water in a saucepan, and stir with a wooden spoon over a medium heat until thickened. Stir in the butter and remove from the heat and allow to cool slightly. Then stir in the beaten eggs, juice, peel and sugar. Return to a very low heat and stir constantly for about 5 minutes or until the mixture thickens substantially. Then spoon the mixture into the ready-made pie shell and chill for at least 3 hours before serving.

Serving suggestion
Serve with whipped cream or on its own.

Serves 7 to 8

Mettai

Guyana

Ingredients
450 g/1 lb plain flour
40 g/1½ oz unsalted butter
2 tablespoons sugar
Cooking oil for frying

Syrup
450 g/1 lb granulated sugar
300 ml/10 fl oz water

Method
Rub the butter into the flour with 2 tablespoons of sugar and then add cold water to make a fairly stiff dough. Roll out on a floured surface in strips of ¼ inch thick and ¼ inch wide. Cut each strip into pieces of about 6 inches long then deep fry until golden. Drain on kitchen paper. For the syrup, dissolve the sugar in cold water over a medium heat, then lower heat and reduce for about 3 minutes or until you have a thickish syrup. Place the mettai into the syrup to coat, lift out with tongs and place on to baking parchment to dry for about 20 minutes before eating. Store in an airtight container for up to two weeks.

Makes about 30

Pineapple Tart

Antigua

Ingredients
1 small pineapple
Sweet shortcrust pastry
230 g/8 oz sugar
300 ml/10 fl oz water

Method
Peel, core and slice the pineapple. Place in a saucepan of water and poach for 10 minutes. Remove and drain the pineapple slices and add sugar to the water and simmer until it thickens. Leave to cool. Line an 8-inch pie tin with pastry and evenly spread the pineapple slices inside, then cover with syrup. Bake in a preheated oven at gas mark 6, 400°F, 200°C, for 45 minutes or until browned.

Serves 4 to 6

Classic Caribbean Cooking

Prune Tart

Dominican Republic

Ingredients
450 g/1 lb pitted prunes
1 unbaked shortcrust pastry shell, 23 cm/9 inch
300 ml/10 fl oz double cream
230 g/8 oz caster sugar
½ teaspoon ground cinnamon
¼ teaspoon salt

Method
Finely chop all but 18 of the prunes. Sift together the flour, salt, sugar and cinnamon. Stir in the cream and chopped prunes and mix well. Turn out into the pastry shell set in a metal flan dish. Place the whole prunes on top and bake in the oven at gas mark 6, 400°F, 200°C, for 30 to 40 minutes or until set.

Serving suggestion
Serve warm with whipped cream or custard flavoured with rum, or vanilla ice cream.

Serves 6

Sweet Plantain Patties

Jamaica

Ingredients
3 very ripe plantains
450 g/1 lb sweet shortcrust pastry
1 tablespoon sugar
1–2 teaspoons vanilla essence, according to taste
¼–½ teaspoon nutmeg, according to taste
Red food colouring (optional)

Method
Boil the plantains in water until they are tender, about 15 minutes, then drain and mash until smooth. Add sugar, vanilla essence, 2 drops of food colouring (if using) and freshly grated nutmeg. Roll out the pastry and cut 8 circles, using a saucer as a guide. Place equal quantities of the plantain mixture on one half of the pastry circles, then fold the other half over and seal with water and crimp the edges. Brush with a little milk and bake on an ungreased baking sheet at gas mark 6, 400°F, 200°C, for 30 minutes or until golden brown.

Serves 8

Bread & Dough

Bammies

Guyana

Ingredients
900 g/2 lb sweet cassava, grated
Unsalted butter or ghee for frying
1 teaspoon salt

Method

Extract the liquid from the grated cassava by wrapping in muslin and squeezing out as much juice as possible. Place the dried cassava in a bowl and mix with salt. Then take enough of the mixture to create individual rounds (bammies), flattened to about the size of a saucer. Melt the butter or ghee in a cast iron frying pan and fry the bammies on both sides until they are dry and brown.

Makes 6 to 8

Bara

Trinidad and Tobago

Ingredients
230 g/8 oz ground split peas
80 g/3 oz flour
1 teaspoon saffron powder
½ teaspoon ground cumin
3 cloves garlic, crushed
1 hot pepper, crushed
1½ teaspoons salt
3 teaspoons baking powder
Oil for frying

Method
Mix the split peas, flour, baking powder, cumin, saffron and salt in a large bowl, and add the garlic and hot pepper. Then add enough water to make a soft dough, cover and set aside for at least half an hour. Take rounded tablespoons of the dough and pat with both hands to flatten to about ¼ inch thick. Fry the baras on each side until cooked and drain on kitchen paper. Serve warm.

Serving suggestion
Serve with mango chutney.

Coconut Bread

Antigua

Ingredients
680 g/1½ lb plain flour
450 g/1 lb sugar
340 g/12 oz fresh coconut, grated, or desiccated equivalent
300 ml/10 fl oz milk
230 g/8 oz seedless raisins
230 g/8 oz butter
2 eggs, size 2
2 teaspoons vanilla extract
2 teaspoons sugar
2 teaspoons baking powder
½ teaspoon salt

Method
Mix cream the butter and sugar together in a large bowl until light and fluffy. Add beaten eggs slowly and mix, then add flour, vanilla, sifted baking powder and salt, beating constantly. Finally, add milk and raisins, then stir well. Turn mixture into a greased 450 g/1 lb loaf tin and sprinkle sugar on top. Bake in a preheated oven at gas mark 3, 325°F, 160°C, for 45 minutes or until golden on top and a knife comes out clean when inserted into the top of the bread.

Serving suggestion
Serve warm or cold, sliced and spread with butter and jam or on its own.

Serves 5

Cornbread

Barbados

Ingredients
300 ml/10 fl oz milk
110 g/4 oz cornmeal
110 g/4 oz plain flour
60 g/2 oz butter
1 egg, size 1
2 tablespoons sugar
1 tablespoon baking powder
½ teaspoon salt

Method
Mix the cornmeal, flour, baking powder, salt and sugar. Add the beaten egg, milk and melted butter to the cornmeal mixture and stir lightly. Half fill a greased pan with the mixture and bake in a preheated oven at gas mark 7, 425°F, 220°C, for 20 to 25 minutes until the bread is lightly brown.

Serves 6

Cornmeal Dumplings

Jamaica

Ingredients
680 g/1½ lb cornmeal
¼ teaspoon nutmeg
1.5 litres/2½ pints cold water
Freshly ground black pepper
Salt

Method
Place water and salt in a large pot and bring to the boil. Add salt, gradually stir in cornmeal, pressing hard after each addition in order to remove the lumps; this should take about 15 minutes. Remove from the pot and add nutmeg and black pepper and shape into small cakes. Drop into a pan of boiling water or soup and cook for a further 10 minutes.

Serving suggestion
Serve with saltfish and callaloo for breakfast or with soup as part of a main course.

Serves 4

Easter Spiced Bun

Jamaica

Ingredients

680 g/1½ lb self raising flour
230 g/8 oz unsalted butter
170 g/6 oz brown sugar
110 g/4 oz glacé cherries
110 g/4 oz currants
110 g/4 oz candied lime peel
110 g/4 oz chopped raisins
300 ml/10 fl oz water

150 ml/5 fl oz milk
1 egg, size 2, beaten
1 yeast cake
1 whole grated nutmeg
1 teaspoon cinnamon
1 teaspoon salt
1 pinch mixed spice

Method

Place the yeast in a small amount of lukewarm water and set aside. Boil water and milk together. Mix beaten egg, sugar, salt, butter and spices in a bowl. Pour in the water and milk. Sift half the flour into the bowl, then pour in the yeast and dried fruit and mix. Add the remainder of the flour to form a stiff dough. Cover with a tea towel and leave in a warm place to rise; depending on the climate, this should take between 30 and 40 minutes. Dough should double in size. Then knead the dough on a clean floured surface for 5 minutes, sprinkle on some more flour and knead again. Shape into two 450 g/1 lb loaves and placed in greased loaf tins. Bake at gas mark 4, 350°F, 180°C, for about 45 minutes or until the bun shrinks from the side of the tin and is springy to the touch.

Serving suggestion

Serve sliced with butter and cheese.

Gingerbread

Jamaica

Ingredients
230 g/8 oz molasses
80 g/3 oz Seville orange marmalade
110 g/4 oz wholemeal flour
110 g/4 oz unsalted butter
60 g/2 oz sugar
150 ml/5 fl oz milk
2 eggs, size 4, well beaten
4 teaspoons fresh ginger, minced
½ teaspoon bicarbonate of soda

Method
Heat butter, sugar, marmalade, molasses and milk together in a pan. Stir gently until sugar dissolves. Allow to cool slightly. Sift flour with salt, soda and spices into a mixing bowl then add wholemeal flour. Add milk mixture to beaten eggs, then pour onto flour. Mix with a wooden spoon until a smooth batter is formed. Pour into an 8 inch square tin and bake at gas mark 3, 325°F, 160°C, for 1½ hours or until gingerbread springs back when pressed. Cool on a wire rack.

Serves 8 to 10

Honey Bread

Jamaica

Ingredients
340 g/12 oz self raising flour
170 g/6 oz Jamaican honey
150 ml/5 fl oz milk
110 g/4 oz soft brown sugar
1 teaspoon salt

Topping
30 g/1 oz Demerara sugar

Method
Sift flour, spice and salt together, then mix in the sugar. Add honey and milk and blend to a smooth, stiff dough. Place dough in a 900 g/2 lb loaf tin and top with sugar. Bake at gas mark 4, 350°F, 180°C, for about 1½ hours, until the top is springy to the touch. Cool before eating.

Serving suggestion
Serve cut into slices with butter for tea or breakfast.

Serves 6

Johnny Cakes

Jamaica

Ingredients
340 g/12 oz plain flour
2 teaspoons butter
1 teaspoon baking powder
¼ teaspoon salt
1 tablespoon cold water
Cooking oil for frying

Method
Sift the flour, baking powder and salt in a large bowl, then rub in the butter as if making pastry. Add sufficient cold water to form a soft but not sticky dough. Flour hands and break off pieces about the size of an egg and shape into rounds. Heat the oil in a frying pan and fry the cakes over a medium heat until both sides are brown and the centre is cooked.

Serving suggestion
Serve hot with butter as a snack or with ackee and saltfish, corned beef hash or fried plantain and bacon and eggs.

Makes 10

Paratha Roti (Buss-up-Shot)

Trinidad and Tobago

Ingredients
450 g/1 lb plain flour
3 teaspoons baking powder
1 teaspoon salt
60 g/2 oz margarine or butter
360 ml/12 fl oz cold water

Method
Sift the flour, baking powder and salt in a large bowl and add water, a little at a time, and combine to form soft but not sticky dough. Remove to a floured work surface and knead for 10 minutes until dough is elastic. Cover and leave to rest for 10 minutes. Divide into 8 balls, then roll out. Coat with margarine or butter and sprinkle with flour. Cut the dough from the centre to the edge and roll tightly into a cone shape, then press the peak of the cone into the centre of the dough and flatten. Leave to stand for another 10 minutes, then return to the floured work surface and roll out the dough very thinly. Bake on a moderately hot tawa (griddle) coating the dough with oil on both sides while cooking, about 1–2 minutes on each side. Remove from the tawa and beat with a wooden palette until flaky, or mash up in a clean cloth until flaky.

Serving suggestion
Serve as an accompaniment to almost any meal.

Sada Roti

Guyana

Ingredients
450 g/1 lb plain flour
3 teaspoons baking powder
1 teaspoon salt
360 ml/12 fl oz cold water

Method
Sift the flour, baking powder and salt in a large bowl and add water, a little at a time, and combine to form soft but not sticky dough. Remove to a floured work surface and knead for 10 minutes until dough is elastic. Cover and leave to rest for 10 minutes. Divide into 8 balls, then roll out to ¼ inch thickness with a rolling pin to form the rotis, and leave to stand for a further 10 minutes. Heat a tawa (griddle) over a medium heat for 3 minutes, then cook the roti on both sides until small blisters appear, do not burn. Wrap rotis in a clean towel and keep warm until all are cooked.

Serving suggestion
Serve hot for breakfast or as a snack.

Serves 4

Spinners

Jamaica

Ingredients
230 g/8 oz plain flour
½ teaspoon baking powder
½ teaspoon salt
150 ml/5 fl oz water

Method
Sift flour, salt and baking powder into a mixing bowl. Add enough cold water to form soft but not sticky dough. Break off small pieces and role in floured hands to form elongated shapes.

Serving suggestion
Add to casseroles, soups, stews and dishes such as stewed peas.

Makes about 15

Sweet Cassava Bread

St Kitts

Ingredients
230 g/8 oz cassava, finely grated
110 g/4 oz coconut, freshly grated
110 g/4 oz brown sugar
1 teaspoon salt

Method
Combine the cassava with salt and leave for 10 minutes, then squeeze out in a clean towel until all the water has gone and cassava is as dry as possible. Spread half the cassava in the bottom of a small heavy baking dish, cover with coconut and brown sugar. Add the remainder of the cassava and bake at gas mark 4, 350°F, 180°C, until lightly browned, about 20 minutes.

Serves 6

Sauce, Dressings & Oils

Coconut Oil

Grenada

Ingredients
4 medium coconuts
300 ml/10 fl oz water

Method
Split the coconuts and extract the flesh. Grate coconut flesh into a bowl, then add water and knead for about 5 minutes to extract the milk. Strain liquid into a saucepan and boil for 1½ hours on a medium heat until liquid turns to oil. Do not stir. Strain, then allow to cool. When cold, pour into a bottle.

Makes 300 ml/10 fl oz

Creole Fish Sauce

Martinique

Ingredients
1 small can tomato puree
1 large green capsicum, finely chopped
1 onion, finely chopped
1 stick celery, finely chopped
1 tablespoon stuffed green olives, finely chopped
½ clove garlic, finely chopped
2 teaspoons hot pepper sauce
1 tablespoon olive oil
1 tablespoon unsalted butter
Salt and freshly ground black pepper

Method
Add the butter to a small saucepan and melt with the olive oil. Then add the capsicum, onion and celery, and soften over a low heat for about 4 minutes, do not allow to caramelise or burn. Add the tomato puree and cook for a further 2 minutes. Add garlic and the remainder of ingredients, and cook on a low heat for 2 more minutes.

Serving suggestion
Serve hot or cold with baked or steamed fish.

Serves 4

Ghee

Trinidad

Ingredients
450 g/1 lb unsalted butter, well chilled

Method
Cut the butter into 6 to 8 pieces and put in a heavy or cast iron saucepan over a medium heat. Melt the butter, stirring occasionally. Bring to the boil and cook for about 1 minute. Reduce heat to the lowest setting and let the butter cook for 40 minutes. The golden oil that remains is ghee. Pour the liquid into a jar through a muslin-lined strainer and store indefinitely in the refrigerator. Use to cook any meat or fish in the same way that you would use oil or butter.

Green Sauce

Cuba

Ingredients
8 tablespoons mayonnaise
4 tablespoons sour cream
2 tablespoons finely chopped watercress
2 teaspoons finely chopped coriander
½ clove garlic, crushed
3 teaspoons hot pepper sauce
½ tablespoon freshly squeezed lime juice

Method
Place all the ingredients in a food processor or blender and blend until all the ingredients have combined, about 30 seconds. Chill and serve with fish or lobster.

Serves 4

Peanut Sauce

St Maarten

Ingredients
6 tablespoons coconut cream
2 tablespoons grated onion
2 tablespoons smooth peanut butter
2 tablespoons extra virgin olive oil
2 teaspoons freshly squeezed lime
2 tablespoons dark brown sugar
Salt and freshly ground pepper

Method
Sauté onions in oil for 5 minutes, then stir in sugar, lime juice and peanut butter. Add coconut cream, salt and pepper and continue stirring until sauce is thick and well blended.

Serving suggestion
Serve with meat or fish, or as a dip with saté

Pork Fat Dressing

Guyana

Ingredients
170 g/6 oz diced belly of pork
½ hot red pepper, de-seeded, chopped
2 tablespoons freshly squeezed lime juice
Salt and freshly ground black pepper

Method
Place the pork in a pan over a low heat and extract all the fat (the fat will melt leaving a clear liquid), then add salt and black pepper. Beat in the lime juice and the chopped pepper and pour over salad.

Spiced Butter Sauce

Guadeloupe

Ingredients
230 g/8 oz unsalted butter
2 spring onions, finely chopped
4 pimento berries, crushed
½ clove garlic, crushed
1 teaspoon curry powder
2 tablespoons freshly squeezed lemon or lime juice
Salt and freshly ground black pepper

Method
Cream the butter with a wooden spoon in a large bowl until butter is soft. Add the other ingredients, one at a time, and beat after every addition. Then place the mixture onto foil or greaseproof paper and flash freeze. When frozen, the butter can be easily sliced into 8 to 10 portions.

Serving suggestion
Serve with steak, or grilled or steamed fish.

Spiced-up Fruit Dressing

Antigua

Ingredients
150 ml/5 fl oz fresh pineapple juice
150 ml/5 fl oz fresh orange juice
Juice of 1 freshly squeezed lime
4 tablespoons tomato ketchup
4 tablespoons mayonnaise
2 tablespoons chopped parsley
Dash hot pepper sauce
Coarsely ground pepper

Method
Combine all the ingredients and use for green or seafood salad.

White Sauce

Ingredients
300 ml/10 fl oz cold full cream milk
60 g/2 oz unsalted butter
30 g/1 oz cornflour
2 teaspoons dry English mustard
Freshly ground white pepper

Method
Melt the butter in a large saucepan, add the mustard and cook for 1 minute. Then add the cornflour and stir constantly for 1 minute. Finally, add the milk and pepper, stirring constantly over a low heat until the sauce thickens.

Serving suggestion
The sauce can be served with fish or you can add cheese, herbs or onion to make a variety of sauces to serve with meat or fish.

Makes 300 ml/10 fl oz

Marinades, Stock & Flavouring

Marinade for Suckling Pig (Adobo)

Cuba

Ingredients
6 tablespoons un-ripe or Seville orange juice
5 tablespoons groundnut oil
½ bulb garlic, peeled and crushed
2 tablespoons fresh oregano, chopped
1 tablespoon fresh sage, chopped
1 tablespoon freshly ground black pepper
2 tablespoons salt

Method
Mix all the ingredients together, coat the pig inside and out with the marinade and leave overnight. The next day, while cooking, baste at regular intervals. This marinade is enough for a pig weighing up to 5.5 kg/12 lb.

Meat Marinade

Guyana

Ingredients
8 slices fresh ginger, minced
2 cloves garlic, peeled and sliced
3 tablespoons vegetable oil
2½ tablespoons dry sherry
2 tablespoons light soy sauce
1 tablespoon dark soy sauce
3 tablespoons cold water
2½ teaspoons sugar
1 teaspoon salt
½ teaspoon white pepper

Method
Place all the ingredients in a large screw-top jar, shake well and refrigerate until required. Use for any red meat dish in Chinese cooking that requires a marinade.

Makes 300 ml/10 fl oz

Poultry Marinade

Guyana

Ingredients
3 tablespoons dry sherry
3 tablespoons vegetable oil
4 slices fresh ginger, minced
½ clove garlic, peeled
3 teaspoons sugar
¼ teaspoon white pepper

Method
Put all the ingredients into a screw-top jar, shake well and refrigerate until required.

Makes 150 ml/5 fl oz

Seafood Marinade

Guyana

Ingredients
8 slices fresh ginger, minced
3 tablespoons dry sherry
1½ teaspoons sugar
½ teaspoon salt
¼ teaspoon white pepper

Method
Combine all the ingredients in a screw-top jar, shake well and refrigerate until required. Use as a marinade in any Chinese dish of fish or seafood.

Makes 150 ml/5 fl oz

Chicken Stock

Ingredients
1 boiling chicken with giblets
2 onions, peeled and sliced
4 stalks celery
2 carrots, peeled and diced
1 thin sliver lemon rind
8 sprigs parsley
1 sprig tarragon
1 sprig thyme
6 peppercorns
1 bay leaf
2.3 litres/4 pints water
2 teaspoons salt

Method
Place cleaned and cut-up chicken and giblets into a large pot with the vegetables. Add the herbs and seasonings, cover with water and bring to the boil, then cover and simmer for 2 hours. Strain and allow to cool. When cold, skim the fat from the surface and use the stock when required. Keep in a refrigerator for up to 3 days, or freeze until needed.

Makes 1.2 litres/2 pints

Fish Stock

Ingredients
450 g/1 lb white fish back bones and skins
2 small carrots, peeled and diced
2 stalks celery
1 onion, sliced
6 sprigs parsley
1 sprig thyme
6 black peppercorns
2 pimentos
1 fresh bay leaf
12 tablespoons white wine (optional)
1.4 litres/2½ pints water
Salt

Method
Put all the ingredients in a large pan or stock pot, bring to the boil and simmer for 30 to 40 minutes or until the liquid has reduced and is well flavoured, then strain. Can be used immediately or cool and freeze until required.

Makes about 1 litre/1¾ pints

Vegetable Stock

Ingredients

3 medium onions
3 medium carrots, peeled and diced
2 leeks (white part only)
1 small turnip, peeled and diced
5 stalks celery
2 slices hot green pepper, de-seeded (optional)
6 peppercorns
6 sprigs parsley
2 sprigs thyme
1 fresh bay leaf
1 tablespoon butter
2.3 litres/4 pints water
Salt and freshly ground white pepper

Method

Cut up all the vegetables and brown these until golden in a little butter. Add water, and bring to the boil then simmer for 1½ hours. Strain and use in stews, soups or sauces. May be frozen and used when required.

Makes 1 litre/1¾ pints

Cassareep

Guyana

Ingredients
2.7 kg/6 lbs cassava root
6 teaspoons Demerera sugar
4 teaspoons caramel colouring
1 teaspoon ground cloves
½ teaspoon ground cinnamon
150 ml/5 fl oz cold water

Method
Peel and grate the cassava. Add the water to the grated root and mix well. Then squeeze out the liquid through fine muslin. Place liquid, sugar and spices into a saucepan, bring to the boil then simmer until liquid is syrupy. Allow to cool, then add caramel colouring. Store in a refrigerator until required to make pepperpot.

Curry Powder

Guyana

Ingredients
2 teaspoons ground coriander
2 teaspoons salt
1 teaspoon chilli powder
1 teaspoon ground ginger
1 teaspoon powdered garlic
½ teaspoon turmeric
½ teaspoon cumin seeds

Method
Mix all the ingredients together and place in an airtight jar. Use in the usual way for seasonings or curries. Vary the strength by adding more or less chilli. The curry powder will last indefinitely.

Makes enough for 450 g/1 lb meat

Garam Masala

Trinidad

Ingredients
6 tablespoons black peppercorns
5 tablespoons coriander seeds
1½ tablespoons green cardamom pods
1½ tablespoons whole cloves
1 tablespoon cumin seeds

Method
Remove cardamom seeds from the pods and place on a baking tray with all the other ingredients. Bake in a very hot oven at gas mark 8, 450°F, 230°C, for 10 minutes, then allow to cool. Grind into a fine powder using a pestle and mortar or electric grinder. Store in an airtight container and use as required. Garam masala will keep fresh for about 6 months.

Sofrito

Puerto Rico

Ingredients
230 g/8 oz diced salt pork
450 g/1 lb tomatoes, skinned and chopped
4 medium onions, finely chopped
2 medium green capsicums, de-seeded and finely chopped
12 cloves garlic, finely chopped
1 tablespoon finely chopped fresh coriander
1 teaspoon dried oregano
Salt and freshly ground black pepper

Method
Fry the salt pork on a low heat in a cast iron or similar heavy frying pan. When meat is brown, lift out and reserve. In the same pan, sauté the onions, garlic and green capsicums until softened, then add the remainder of the ingredients, including the pork. Simmer on a low heat for 30 minutes. Allow to cool, then place in jars and refrigerate until required.

Makes about 340 g/12 oz

Chutney,
Pickles
& Jam

Mango Chutney

Trinidad

Ingredients
12 un-ripe mangoes, thinly sliced
900 g/2 lb brown sugar
600 ml/1 pint malt vinegar
6 medium onions, thinly sliced
1 hot pepper
110 g/4 oz seedless raisins
2 tablespoons melted butter
12 cloves
1 stick cinnamon
1 fresh bay leaf
2.5 cm/1 inch peeled ginger
1 teaspoon salt

Method
Tie all the spices together in a piece of muslin. Next, dissolve sugar, salt and vinegar in a cast iron or preserving pan, then add the spices and all the remaining ingredients and simmer for 15 minutes. Cool, then place in sterilised jars, cover and seal. Leave for 4 weeks so that the flavours mature.

Serving suggestion
Serve with curries, cheese, fish and meats.

Makes 2.7 kgs/6 lbs

Lime Pickle

Guyana

Ingredients
12 limes
300 ml/10 fl oz olive oil
3 tablespoons chilli powder
3 tablespoons salt
1 tablespoon mustard seeds
1 tablespoon turmeric
1 tablespoon fenugreek

Method
Cut each lime into 6 sections and remove the pips. Place the limes in a large preserving jar, cover with salt and set aside. Dry roast the fenugreek and mustard seeds then grind to a fine powder. Add the ground seeds, chilli powder and turmeric to the limes and mix well. Heat the oil, then pour over the limes and mix well. Cover with a cloth and leave the limes in a warm place for 10 to 15 days until the limes are soft and they have turned brown. Store in sterilised preserving jars. This will keep indefinitely and is ready to eat after 15 days.

Serving suggestion
Serve with curries, meat or fish.

Makes 450 g/1 lb

Author's note: To dry roast add the ingredients to a small frying pan without oil and heat gently on a low heat until the spices begin to change colour and the aroma is released, stir frequently.

Pickled Vegetables

Dominican Republic

Ingredients
230 g/8 oz whole green beans, chopped into 1 cm/½ inch pieces
230 g/8 oz white cabbage, finely shredded
230 g/8 oz fresh green peas
1 medium onion, finely chopped
1 hot red pepper, sliced and de-seeded
White wine vinegar

Method
Place equal amounts of vegetables in sterilised jars, cover with vinegar and replace lids. Store in the refrigerator for 2 weeks before eating.

Serving suggestion
Serve with meat or fish.

Banana Jam

St Lucia

Ingredients
8 bananas, medium ripe
680 g/1½ lb preserving sugar
Juice of 3 freshly squeezed limes
300 ml/10 fl oz water

Method
Place the sugar, water and lime juice in a large preserving pan or cast iron pan and bring to the boil. Chop bananas, then add to the pan. Simmer for 45 minutes or until jam thickens. Cool slightly then transfer to 2 sterilised 450 g/1 lb jars. When cold, cover and seal. Leave for 1 month for flavours to mature before eating.

Sorrel Jam

Jamaica

Ingredients
900 g/2 lb sorrel petals
1.3 kg/3 lb preserving sugar
750 ml/1¼ pints water

Method
Wash the sorrel several times to ensure that dirt and grit are removed. Place sorrel and water in a large preserving pan or heavy saucepan and boil for 25 minutes until tender. Add the sugar, stir well and simmer for 35 minutes or until it gels. When tested in cold water, transfer to warm sterilised jars. Leave for at least a week to mature.

Makes 1.8 kg/4 lbs

Tomato Jam

Dominica

Ingredients
450 g/1 lb small ripe tomatoes
450 g/1 lb brown sugar
2.5 cm/1 inch cinnamon bark
½ vanilla pod, split

Method
Wash and cut tomatoes lengthways and remove seeds. Place sugar in a cast iron or preserving pan with spices and 150 ml/5 fl oz of water and boil. When all the sugar has dissolved add tomatoes and boil quickly to set, this should take about 15 minutes. Cool then bottle in sterilised jars. Seal with grease proof paper and label jars. Use after 2 weeks .

Serving suggestion
Serve with cold meats, fish or cheese.

Guava Jelly

Jamaica

Ingredients
900 g/2 lb fresh guavas
1.3 kg/3 lb preserving sugar
5 g/¼ oz citric acid
750 ml/1¼ pints water

Method
Chop the guavas and cover with water in a large saucepan or preserving pan. Boil until the guavas are soft enough to puree. Strain through a jelly bag overnight. The following day, add sugar to the liquid and boil to setting point. Cool, then stir in the citric acid, pour into warm sterilised jars. Store and use as required.

Makes 6 pounds

Author's note: Jelly bags are available from specialist cook shops, otherwise use fine muslin.

Ortanique Marmalade

Jamaica

Ingredients
1.8 kg/4 lb ortaniques (see Glossary)
1.8 kg/4 lb preserving sugar

Method
Wash and halve the fruit and squeeze the juice into a bowl and refrigerate. Remove and discard all the pith and membranes from the ortaniques. Place the rind in a large saucepan, cover with cold water and simmer for 20 minutes until tender. Drain and discard the water, then place the peel in a clean bowl, cover and refrigerate overnight, changing the water 4 times to remove the bitterness. The next day, drain the peel and place in a large preserving pan. Cut the peel into 2.5 cm/1 inch strips, add sugar and the juice, bring to the boil, then simmer for 40 minutes or until the marmalade is set when dropped into cold water. A jam thermometer will help with this process. While still warm place the marmalade in warm sterilised jars, seal and store for 1 month before consuming.

Makes about 2.7 kg/6 lbs

Drinks

Anisette

Dominica

Ingredients
600 ml/1 pint white rum
450 g/1 lb dark brown sugar
1 bundle anise
2 cups water

Method
Place anise and rum in a large bottle and cork. Leave for 3 days. Prepare sugar syrup by combining sugar and water together in a saucepan, then on a low heat, stirring constantly, mix until sugar has dissolved. Cool, then add rum and anise to the syrup. Strain through a fine tea strainer, bottle and re-cork. Leave for 1 month in a cool dark place before consuming.

Serves 6 to 8

Aunt Carrie's Rice Wine

Guyana

Ingredients
1.3 kg/3 lb Demerara sugar
110 g/4 oz long grain white rice
60 g/2 oz raisins
30 g/1 oz fresh yeast
10 g/½ oz cloves
1 large orange
3 to 4 pieces mace
1 cinnamon stick, about 6 cm/1½ inches long
2.2 litres/4 pints water

Method
Cut the orange into quarters, leaving the rind on the fruit. Wash the rice and discard the water. Place all the ingredients into a large stone jar which holds at least 2.3 litres/4 pints of water. Stir until the sugar has dissolved. Cover and leave for 5 days. Strain and re-bottle in a tightly covered jar for 21 days. If possible, use wine bottles as a second fermentation may take place. It is ready for drinking after 21 days.

Serves 20

Bahamas Punch

Bahamas

Ingredients
3 measures Bacardi
1 slice fresh lemon
1 slice fresh orange
2 drops Angostura Bitters
Juice of 1 fresh lemon
1 teaspoon sugar syrup
½ teaspoon grenadine
¼ teaspoon freshly grated nutmeg
Cracked ice

Method
Chop up all the fruit, place in a large jug and add rum, sugar syrup, grenadine and bitters. Stir and refrigerate for up to 3 hours. Fill a glass with cracked ice and pour in the mixture. Sprinkle grated nutmeg on top and serve.

Serves 1

Author's note: If you do not have an ice crusher, place ice cubes in a clean tea towel and crush with a rolling pin. Then apply a rolling motion until the ice is well broken.

Banana Fruit Punch

St Lucia

Ingredients
4 ripe bananas
750 ml/1¼ pints freshly squeezed orange juice
240 ml/8 fl oz freshly squeezed lime juice
230 g/8 oz sugar
750 ml/1¼ pints water
½ teaspoon grated nutmeg

Method
Peel the bananas, then place all the ingredients into a blender or juicer and blend until combined, about 40 seconds. Serve over crushed ice.

Serves 10

Banana Milkshake

Jamaica

Ingredients
3 to 4 medium ripe bananas
1 litre/1¾ pints milk
300 ml/10 fl oz vanilla ice cream
110 g/4 oz caster sugar

Method
Place all the ingredients in a food processor or blender and whiz for 1 minute. Pour into a glass and serve immediately.

Serves 4

Barbados Punch

Barbados

Ingredients
3 measures Mount Gay rum
Juice of 1 freshly squeezed orange
Juice of 1 freshly squeezed lime
3 drops Angostura Bitters
1 teaspoon sugar syrup
1 wedge fresh pineapple
1 slice fresh orange
¼ teaspoon freshly grated nutmeg
Cracked ice

Method
Pour all the ingredients into a large glass jug, with the exception of the ice, nutmeg and slice of orange. Stir well and refrigerate for up to 3 hours. Then place cracked ice in a tall glass and pour in the drink. Decorate with a slice of orange and freshly grated nutmeg.

Serves 1

Brown Cow

Jamaica

Ingredients
120 ml/4 fl oz Tia Maria, or similar liqueur
120 ml/4 fl oz evaporated milk
1 roasted coffee bean, ground
Crushed ice

Method
Mix Tia Maria and evaporated milk together. Place in a cocktail shaker and shake well for about 40 seconds. Pour into a tall glass over crushed ice. Decorate with a dusting of ground roasted coffee beans, and serve.

Serves 1

Carrot Drink

Jamaica

Ingredients
6 large carrots, grated
6 tablespoons fresh lime juice
750 g/1¼ pints water
Sugar to taste

Method
Mix together the grated carrots and water, then squeeze through muslin or strain. Add lime juice and sugar to taste. Mix again and serve over ice cubes.

Serves 5

Author's note: There are several variations on this drink. Some people prefer to withhold the lime and add evaporated or condensed milk in place of the water. The healthy option is to follow the recipe and omit the sugar. A juicer will extract the best juice and help retain more of the nutrients.

Cocoa

Dominica

Ingredients
1 cup coconut milk
4 sticks cocoa
1 vanilla pod
1 small sprig anise
½ teaspoon cinnamon powder
½ teaspoon grated nutmeg
1.2 litres/2 pints water

Method
Grate or break cocoa sticks. Boil in 300 ml/10 fl oz of water, add nutmeg, vanilla and anise. When cocoa has melted add remaining water and coconut milk. Bring to the boil and serve.

Serves 4

Author's note: Add sugar to further sweeten if required.

Coconut Drink

Grenada

Ingredients
1 medium coconut
110 g/4 oz sugar
½ teaspoon vanilla essence
750 g/1¼ pints water

Method
Break the coconut and reserve the liquid. Grate coconut flesh and add to the water. Mix well, then strain through a sieve. Add the coconut liquid to the mixture, then add the vanilla essence. Serve over crushed ice.

Serves 4

Coconut Sparkle

Jamaica

Ingredients
300 ml/10 fl oz coconut water
2 measures dark Jamaican rum
1 measure pimento liqueur
Juice of 1 freshly squeezed lime
1 slice lime
1 slice orange
Crushed ice

Method
Place all the ingredients, except the lime and orange slices, into a cocktail shaker and shake well for two minutes. Pour into a tall glass and decorate with the slices of lime and orange, and serve.

Serves 1

Cuba Libra

Cuba

Ingredients
2 measures dark Cuban rum
Juice of ½ a medium lime
½ can cola

Method
Half fill a tumbler with ice cubes. Add the lime juice and rum then stir. Top up with cola and decorate with twisted slices of lime on the side of the glass. Ice cubes may be added at the last moment, then serve.

Serves 1

Dragon Jim

Jamaica

Ingredients
600 ml/1 pint Dragon Stout
110 g/4 oz malt
120 ml/4 fl oz sugar syrup
4 scoops vanilla ice cream

Method
Blend ice cream, malt and sugar syrup for 1 minute, gradually add stout and blend for two more minutes. Serve in a tall glass with ice cubes.

Serves 1

El Jibaro

Puerto Rico

Ingredients
60 ml/2 fl oz freshly squeezed orange juice
60 ml/2 fl oz freshly squeezed lemon juice
60 ml/2 fl oz dark rum
30 ml/1 fl oz over-proof white rum
3 drops Grand Marnier
1 slice lime
3 ice cubes
Mint leaves

Method
Place orange and lemon juices, and dark rum into a cocktail shaker and shake for 2 minutes. Strain into a tall glass and add ice. Pour in Grand Marnier and white rum and decorate with mint leaves and a slice of lime, then serve.

Serves 1

Frozen Daiquiri

Cuba

Ingredients
90 ml/3 fl oz light Cuban rum
2 tablespoons freshly squeezed lime juice
2 teaspoons caster sugar
230 g/8 oz crushed ice

Method
Place all the ingredients in a food processor or high speed blender and whiz until the contents have the consistency of snow. Serve immediately in a champagne glass.

Serves 1

Author's note: From this traditional recipe other fruits, such as bananas and strawberries, are used to make interesting variations of the original recipe.

Ginger Beer

Guyana

Ingredients
1.3 kg/3 lb sugar
230 g/8 oz fresh ginger, peeled and grated
110 g/4 oz uncooked white rice
4.5 litres/8 pints cold water
Juice of ½ lime
6 cloves

Method
Mix all the ingredients together and stir until the sugar has dissolved. Place the mixture into 2 or 3 large jars, cover and leave for 2 days in a warm dark place. On the third day, strain and bottle the liquid. Serve with ice.

Makes approximately 30 servings

Grapefruit and Grenadine Fizz

The Grenadines

Ingredients
600 ml/1 pint freshly squeezed grapefruit juice
300 ml/10 fl oz soda water
150 ml/5 fl oz grenadine
Sugar to taste

Method
Combine all the ingredients and blend for 30 seconds. Pour
into a jug and refrigerate for 30 minutes. Serve over crushed ice.

Serves 3

Grenada Cocktail

Grenada

Ingredients
1 measure sweet Italian vermouth
Juice of ½ a freshly squeezed orange
Powdered cinnamon
3 measures Grenadian rum
5 ice cubes

Method
Pour rum, vermouth and orange juice into a glass jug, add ice cubes and stir well. Strain and pour into a chilled martini glass. Sprinkle cinnamon on top and serve immediately.

Serves 1

Limeade

Dominica

Ingredients
310 g/11 oz caster sugar
240 ml/8 fl oz freshly squeezed lime juice
1.4 litres/2½ pints water

Method
Put all the ingredients in a large jug and stir well until sugar has dissolved. Usually, limeade is made with brown sugar but it takes longer to dissolve than caster sugar, so it really is up to the individual. Chill and serve with ice cubes.

Serves 9 to 10

Mango Crush

Jamaica

Ingredients
10 large ripe mangoes
450 g/1 lb sugar
Juice of 2 freshly squeezed limes
3.4 litres/6 pints water

Method
Peel the mangoes and remove the stones. Puree mango flesh in a blender, food processor or sieve. Mix the puree with water, sugar and lime. Chill, then serve over crushed ice.

Serves 6

Mauby

Guyana

Ingredients
900 g/2 lb brown sugar
30 g/1 oz mauby bark (see Glossary)
600 ml/1 pint soda water
8 cloves
3 bay leaves
2 blades mace
1 cinnamon stick, about 5 cm/2 inches long
1 vanilla pod
½ rind of an orange
2.3 litres/4 pints cold water, for mixing
600 ml/1 pint water

Method
Place the mauby bark, cinnamon stick, cloves, bay, leaves, mace and orange peel in a large saucepan. Add 1 pint of water, then simmer on a low heat until the liquid has reduced by a third and the colour is dark. Put sugar in a large pan and pour on the hot liquid. Retain the spices, add a split vanilla pod and more water, re-boil for 5 minutes then add the water to the pan. Stir well. When the sugar has dissolved, add another 2.3 litres/4 pints of water and the soda water, mix thoroughly then brew for 6 minutes. The mauby will then start to ferment. When this happens let it stand for another 10 minutes. Taste and adjust sweetness. Serve cold over plenty of ice.

Serves 10 to 12

Author's note: Mauby bark is available from specialist Caribbean and Asian food shops

Peanut Punch

Trinidad

Ingredients
7 tablespoons smooth peanut butter
450 ml/15 fl oz full cream milk
2 tablespoons arrowroot
Caster sugar to taste
150 ml/5 fl oz water

Method
Blend the arrowroot with the water then pour into a medium saucepan and combine with milk, peanut butter and sugar to the sweetness required. Whisk the ingredients together over a moderate heat until the mixture is well blended and thickened. Remove from heat, then cool and refrigerate until required. Serve with ice.

Serves 2

Pina Colada

Puerto Rico

Ingredients
3 measures Puerto Rican rum
3 tablespoons coconut milk
3 tablespoons crushed fresh pineapple
1 slice fresh pineapple
2 cups crushed ice

Method
Blend all the ingredients, except the pineapple slice, for 30 seconds. Strain into a tall glass and serve with a straw and a slice of pineapple on the side of the glass.

Serves 1

Pina Fria

Dominican Republic

Ingredients
2 measures white rum
1 measure pineapple juice
2 drops Angostura bitters
4 ice cubes

Method
Put the ice cubes into a cocktail shaker, pour in the rum, bitters and pineapple juice and shake well. Strain into a small glass tumbler.

Serves 1

Pineappleade

Antigua

Ingredients
1 medium pineapple
450 g/1 lb sugar
150 ml/5 fl oz freshly squeezed lime juice
3 pints water

Method
Peel and core the pineapple, cut into slices then grate or shred finely in a processor. Place in a bowl and pour lime juice over. Boil sugar with 450 ml/15 fl oz of water for 4 minutes, and then pour onto fruit. Add remaining water, mix well, then strain and press fruit to extract juices. Serve with ice. Can also be used as a mixer with rum or any other alcoholic drink.

Makes 3 pints

Pink Bacardi

Bahamas

Ingredients
3 measures Bacardi
Juice of 1 freshly squeezed lime
5 drops grenadine
1 teaspoon sugar
5 ice cubes

Method
Place all the ingredients in a cocktail shaker and shake until frost forms on the outside. Strain and pour into a chilled martini glass.

Serves 1

Punch Vieux

Martinique

Ingredients
40 g/1½ oz rhum vieux
10 g/½ oz cane juice or sugar cane syrup
Water

Method
Pour the rhum and cane juice or syrup in a small glass, add water to your taste and stir gently.

Serves 1

Author's note: If you are unable to obtain cane syrup or cane juice, use sugar syrup.

Rum Collins

Jamaica

Ingredients
2 measures Appleton dark rum
Juice of 1 freshly squeezed lime
1 teaspoon caster sugar
1 slice lime
1 cocktail cherry
10 ice cubes
Soda water

Method
Place 5 ice cubes in a cocktail shaker, add all the ingredients with the exception of the lime slice, cocktail cherry and soda water. Shake for 1 minute then strain into a tall glass that has the remainder of the ice cubes in it. Top up with soda water. Thread lime and cherry onto a cocktail stick and serve with a straw.

Serves 1

Rum Curaçao

Curaçao

Ingredients
3 measures light rum
1 measure curaçao
3 drops Angostura Bitters
1 slice fresh orange rind
5 ice cubes

Method
Put the ice cubes into a cocktail shaker. Shake the bitters over the ice, next pour in the rum and curaçao. Shake until frost forms. Strain and pour into a short tumbler. Decorate with a slice of orange rind and serve.

Serves 1

Sanguire

Dominica

Ingredients
1 bottle claret
60 g/2 oz cinnamon
¼ teaspoon freshly grated nutmeg
1 litre/1¾ pints water
Sugar to taste

Method
Boil water and spice in an enamel saucepan and reduce until you have 600 ml/1 pint of liquid remaining. Remove from heat and add the claret. Sweeten to taste. Pour into wine glasses when slightly cooled. Sprinkle with grated nutmeg.

Serves 6 to 8

Sea Moss Drink

Dominica

Ingredients
10 g/½ oz sea moss (see Glossary)
1 freshly squeezed lime
1 cm/½ inch cinnamon bark
¼ teaspoon freshly grated nutmeg
1 litre/1¾ pints water
Milk as required
Sugar to taste

Method
Wash the sea moss and soak in water overnight. Strain the sea moss and place in a saucepan with the water and lime juice. Boil for two hours over a medium heat. For every cup of strained melted sea moss, add ½ cup of milk. Boil again with nutmeg and cinnamon, add sugar to taste.

Serves 4

Shrub

Guadeloupe

Ingredients
1 bottle rhum vieux
4 Seville oranges
110 g/4 oz granulated sugar
3 tablespoons water

Method
Pour out 2½ measures of rhum from the bottle. Peel skins off the oranges as thinly as possible. Next, boil the sugar with the water in a small saucepan until the sugar has dissolved. Cool then pour the syrup and the chopped peel into the rhum bottle and replace the cork and leave in a cool dark place for 3 weeks. Strain and re-bottle. This drink is served as a liqueur.

Sorrel Wine

Guyana

Ingredients
900 g/2 lb sugar
450 g/1 lb sorrel petals
3 to 4 blades mace
2.3 g/4 pints water

Method
Place all the ingredients into a sterile jar then stir well until sugar has dissolved. Cover tightly with brown paper, doubled and tied with string around the neck of the jar. Leave for 21 days, then strain into sterile wine bottles. The sorrel petals have natural yeast so second fermentation may occur. Check regularly, especially if wine is stored in a warm place as it could be ready after 15 days.

Serves 20

Soursop Punch

Jamaica

Ingredients
3 medium soursop
1.4 litres/2½ pints full cream milk
¼ teaspoon freshly grated nutmeg
1.4 litres/2½ pints water

Method
Remove the skin and core from the soursops. Chop the flesh, then add to the water. Mix well and then squeeze through a fine muslin cloth or sieve. Add the strained liquid to the milk, nutmeg and enough sugar to your taste. Chill and serve with ice.

Serves 6

St Lucia Cocktail

St Lucia

Ingredients
2 measures white rum
1 measure curacao
1 measure dry French vermouth
1 teaspoon grenadine
Juice of ½ a freshly squeezed orange

Method
Place ice cubes into a cocktail shaker and add rum, orange juice, grenadine, curacao and vermouth. Shake until frost forms and pour into a tall glass. Decorate with a slice of orange.

Serves 1

Tobago Punch

Tobago

Ingredients
3 measures golden rum
½ teaspoon grenadine
3 drops Angostura Bitters
Juice of 1 freshly squeezed orange
Juice of 1 freshly squeezed lime
1 slice fresh pineapple
1 slice fresh lime
1 slice fresh orange
1 teaspoon sugar syrup
¼ teaspoon freshly grated nutmeg
Cracked ice

Method
Pour the fruit juices into a jug, add syrup, bitters, grenadine, sliced fruits and rum. Stir and store in the refrigerator for up to 3 hours. Fill a glass with cracked ice and pour the punch and fruits into it. Decorate with grated nutmeg.

Serves 1

Zombie

Haiti

Ingredients
1 measure Haitian dark rum
1 measure Haitian white rum
1 measure pineapple juice
1 teaspoon sugar

Method
Shake all the ingredients well for about 1 minute in a cocktail shaker with ice cubes. Strain into a tall glass. Decorate with pieces of pineapple threaded on to a cocktail stick and laid on top of the glass and serve.

Serves 1

Glossary

Ackee, Akee, Achee: The fruit of a sapindaceous tree, *bligha sapida*, named after Captain Bligh who introduced the tree into the Caribbean from west Africa. The yellow fruit, which is contained in a scarlet shell, has a shiny black seed. It is widely eaten in Jamaica in a variety of dishes including the famous ackee and saltfish, in patties, as stuffing for breadfruit and as a base for soup. It must be cooked before consumption. Outside of the Caribbean, it is available in cans.

Agar-Agar: A setting agent used in Chinese cooking which is an ideal alternative to gelatine for vegans and vegetarians. It can be purchased in many supermarkets and Chinese and Japanese food shops.

Allspice: See Pimento

Angostura Bitters: An aromatic liquid used to enhance the flavour of alcoholic drinks, especially punches.

Anise, Star: An eight pointed clove with a strong aroma of aniseed. It is favoured in Chinese cooking and can be used whole or ground to make Five Spiced Powder.

Annatto: *Bixa orellana*. The seeds of a small flowering tree that are used to colour and flavour food. Annatto oil is commonly used in Caribbean cooking and comes from the orange pulp that surrounds the seeds. It is available in both seed and oil form and can be obtained from many specialist food shops.

Arrowroot: *Marinate arundinacea*. The rhizomes (root-like plant stems) yield an easily digestible, nutritious starch which is widely used as a thickening agent. It is sold in packets in most food shops.

Aubergine, Garden Egg: See Eggplant

Avocado: *Persea Americana*. This was first cultivated in Mexico circa 7000 BC but is now widely cultivated in tropical and semi-tropical climates. The Caribbean avocado is usually large pear-shaped and dark green. It can be stuffed, sliced for salads, used in dips and spreads, and eaten raw or cooked.

Blue Mountain Coffee: Regarded by connoisseurs as the best in the world, and one of the most expensive. Grown in the eastern part of Jamaica, in the Blue Mountain range of hills, it is used as the basis for the well-known liqueur, Tia Maria. It was first introduced from Hispaniola in 1728 but was later planted by the freed slaves after the abolition of slavery in Jamaica in 1838. Jamaican coffee is mild and smooth. Only coffee grown and harvested in the Blue Mountains carries the name.

Bouquet Garni: A French term, which, literally translated, means garnished bouquet. It is a bunch of fresh herbs tied together and added to marinades, soups and stews, usually consisting of a bay leaf, parsley, thyme and sometimes celery. It is buried in the liquid and removed before serving.

Breadfruit: The large green fruit of the *artocarpus communis* tree, or breadfruit tree. This large tree was originally cultivated in the south Pacific and was introduced to Jamaica and St Vincent by Captain Bligh in 1793, where the original plant is still growing in the botanical gardens. Now widely grown and exported both fresh and canned, it has a variety of uses. Usually the fruit is peeled and cooked by boiling or roasting. Often it is stuffed with meat or fish, mashed like potatoes, added to stews or turned into soup. The fruit of the tree is round or lantern-shaped and can weigh up to 4.5 kgs/10 lbs. It has a greenish-yellow pitted skin, yellowish-white flesh, and either black or white seeds.

Cacao: *Theobroma cacao.* A small tropical evergreen tree with yellowish flowers and reddish-brown seed pods from which chocolate and cocoa are made. It was introduced to the Caribbean from west Africa.

Callaloo, Calaloo, Callalou: *Colocasia esculenta or xanthosoma sagittisolium.* The collective name refers to a variety of plants which come from Indian kale, or the taro or eddo. More commonly made into soups, the leaves are also cooked with saltfish and used to stuff whole fish or served with egg dishes in much the same way as spinach or Swiss chard would be used. It also has a similar taste and appearance. It can be bought fresh from markets selling Indian and Caribbean foodstuffs, or canned from many specialist shops.

Capsicum: *Capsicum frutescens.* A tropical American pepper of the solanaceous genus, having mild or pungent seeds enclosed in a bell-shaped fruit. It is used as a vegetable or ground to produce a pepper. Can be eaten when they are green, red, or yellow. Mostly used as flavouring and seasoning for savoury dishes, but may be stuffed with meat, fish, rice or other vegetables.

Cassareep: The juice of the bitter cassava root, boiled down and used especially in Guyanese pepperpot and as flavouring in other dishes.

Cassava, Manioc, Yucca: *Manihot esculenta or manihot dulcis* represents bitter and sweet cassava respectively. It is a starch, which is derived from the root of the plant that is used to make tapioca. It looks like a long dark brown hairy root; the bitter variety must always be cooked before eating. Cassava meal is used to make bread and cakes. It can be grated or used much like any other starchy root vegetable. In the French Caribbean, cassava meal is often sold as farine de manioc.

Cho-Cho, Christophene, Chayote: *Sechium edule.* Also known as tropical squash. It is light green with a somewhat prickly skin and a single edible seed. It is used in a variety of dishes throughout the Caribbean, and makes a good addition to soup and casseroles. It can be used in pickles and is sometimes substituted for apples in pies.

Coconut: *Cocos nucifera.* The fruit of a tall palm tree. It is widely planted throughout the Caribbean. The coconut is extremely versatile. When green it contains coconut water, a very refreshing drink and the kernel is a jelly-like substance, which is also edible. When matured, the fruit is contained in a thin dark brown hairy shell. The hollow centre is filled with coconut milk. The white meat is used in curries, and when shredded it is used in cakes. It can be processed into a cream, which is also used in sweet and savoury dishes. Coconut milk is often canned and used in sauces and ice creams and desserts as well as savoury dishes. It is a valuable source of iron and phosphorous. An essential ingredient of many Caribbean dishes.

Conch, Concha, Conque: *Strombus gigas,* tropical marine gastropod molluscs, characterised by a large brightly coloured spiral shell. The pinkish-grey meat is eaten in soups, stews, fritters and salads. It is very tough and has to be pounded and well marinated before eating. Lambi is the Carib name for conch and is referred to by its original name in many of the Caribbean countries.

Coriander, Culantro, Cilantro, Culantrill, Coriandre: *Coriandrum sativum:* This is widely used as a flavouring herb or fresh as a garnish in many countries in the Caribbean, especially the Spanish-speaking islands. It is also used widely by the Syrian community of Jamaica, and by the Indian communities as an addition to curries and chutneys. It can be ground and added to stews or soups, or used as stuffing for meats and fish or in place of parsley as a garnish. In its raw state, it resembles flat leaf parsley but it has a peppery flavour. It is available fresh, ground or in seed form.

Crapaud: This is a variety of large frog, often known as Mountain Chicken, and found in Montserrat and Dominica. An ideal substitute outside of the Caribbean would be the variety of frog used in France.

Crayfish, Langosta, Langouste, Rock Lobster: *Genera astacus and cambarus.* Resembles a small lobster. The meat is contained in the tail and differs from the lobster in that it does not have large claws. It is cooked and served as lobster, in soups, stews, and salads and with a variety of sauces.

Curaçao: This is an alcoholic beverage originally made from the bitter oranges of the Dutch island of Curaçao. Used as a liqueur or added to fruit, desserts and cocktails as a flavouring.

Dhal, Dal: Means chickpea in Trinidad and Tobago but is the Hindi word for any and all legumes, including lentils. Often referred to as gram or channa, it is a prominent feature of Indian-Caribbean cookery.

Dasheen, Taro: *Colocasia esculenta.* The young leaves are known as callaloo but the older root, which can weigh up to 2.3 kgs/5 lbs is edible and is roasted, boiled and served in place of yam or potatoes. It can also be added to soups and stews. The roots are covered in a dark brown skin and are rich in potassium and fibre.

Eddo: See Dasheen

Eggplant, Berenjena, Belangere: *Solanum melongena* is widely cultivated throughout the Caribbean and is cooked in a variety of ways. It is a favoured addition to curries and stews. It is also fried and served as an accompaniment to meat and fish and is used in dips and chutneys. It is sold in most greengrocers and markets and is usually identified by its dark purple colour and egg shape.

Five Spice Powder: This is a strong seasoning used in Chinese cuisine. It comprises equal parts of brown peppercorns (fagara), cinnamon bark, fennel, clove and star anise. All the spices are ground to a fine consistency.

Ginger: *Zingiber officinale.* Now widely cultivated throughout the Caribbean, especially Jamaica, this root spice was native to south-east Asia. It is extensively used in Caribbean cooking. Many Chinese and Indian dishes use ginger root as an important flavouring for meat and fish dishes, chutneys, relishes and jams. Ginger is also used to make drinks, like wine, beer and tea, which is particularly good for aiding digestion. It is also a favoured spice for cakes, bread and biscuits. It has a pale yellowish-brown skin and is knobbly in appearance. It should be peeled before use.

Grenadine: A syrup which is made from pomegranate juice. It is sweet and is used frequently in both fruit and rum-based drinks. Its pinkish-red colour makes it both distinctive and pleasant to ingest.

Guava: *Psidium guajava.* A fruit rich in vitamin C and vitamin A. They can be eaten raw or cooked in a number of ways. Eaten stewed as a dessert, cooked to make jelly or jam or added to drinks to make both non-alcoholic and alcoholic punches and wine. The fruit is green and turns yellow when ripe; the flesh is white, pink or dark pink. Guavas are available fresh or canned.

Gungo Peas: See Pigeon Peas

Hearts of Palm, Palmito, Chou Palmiste: These are the tender hearts of several species of palm trees, much favoured for use in salads or fritters, sometimes served as a starter with a sauce or as an accompaniment to a main course. They are sold fresh in many parts of the Caribbean. Elsewhere, they are usually available canned in salted water, which must be drained before use.

Irish Moss, Carageen: It is a red algae found in tropical waters and Ireland, hence one of its names. It is rich in potassium, calcium, protein and iodine. It has a number of medicinal uses such as treating intestinal problems, as a bulk laxative and for coughs and bronchitis. There are many claims associated with this natural product including cures for tuberculosis and increasing vitality and stamina. It is frequently made into ice cream, puddings and drinks. Outside of Ireland and the Caribbean it may be purchased in markets and specialists shops but is usually found as a ready-made drink or as an additive to prepared sweets and foodstuffs.

Lambi, Lambie: See Conch

Mango: *Mangifera indica.* Mangoes where introduced into the Caribbean in the late 17th century from south-east Asia. The mango tree grows to a height of up to 60 feet. The fruit may vary in colour from orange, pink, and yellow to green with red spots. Peeled, the fruit inside is usually yellow-orange with a large stone inside. The mango is used in a many ways, namely chutneys, pickles, as a fruit served on its own, ice-creams, drinks, desserts, stewed and when under-ripe it may be cooked and added to curries. The mango is rich in vitamins A, B1 and C, making it an extremely healthy addition to any diet.

Mauby, Mawby, Mabi: *Colubrina elliptica or colubrina arborescens.* Mauby is the name given to a bittersweet drink made from the bark of the rhamnaceous tree. It can be mixed with orange and other juices and served over cracked or crushed ice. Nowadays, it is available to buy ready-made, leaving only sugar and juices to be added according to taste.

Melongene: See Eggplant

Nutmeg: *Myristica fragrans.* As spice that originated in south-east Asia, but is now associated with the island of Grenada. Although nutmeg is grown throughout the Caribbean, many regard Grenadian nutmeg as the best. It has a pretty flower, which bears hard brown shell fruit. It can be grated and added to a variety of drinks, desserts and savoury dishes. It is available from shops in powdered form or as whole nutmeg to grate as required.

Okra, Ladies' Fingers, Bamie, Molondron, Quingombo, Gombo: *Hibiscus esculentus.* Originally cultivated in west Africa, but now very much a favourite ingredient in stews and soups in Asian cuisine as well as African, Caribbean and in the southern states of the USA. It is an annual malvaceous plant with yellow-red flowers and a long sticky green edible pod. May be served as a side dish to accompany meat or fish dishes but is more commonly served in curries, soups and stews.

Ortanique: A fruit which was wholly developed in Jamaica. It is a cross between an orange and tangerine, with a thin tough skin and slightly larger than a tangerine. It is very sweet, rich in vitamin C and can be substituted for oranges, satsumas or tangerines. It is ideal for juicing or eating and can be made into marmalade. Its season is comparatively short but is well worth the time and trouble to find in greengrocers, markets or supermarkets.

Papaya, Pawpaw: *Carica papaya.* The fruit of a large evergreen tree. The leaves are used to wrap meat which is then boiled; the leaves then produce the enzyme papuan, a natural tenderiser. The fruit, when ripe, is yellowish orange. It can be eaten on its own, when de-seeded, or as part of a fruit salad. It is also made into jellies, ice-creams, sauces or drinks. The fruit, when under-ripe, is often added to chutneys or pickles and sometimes cooked in curries. It is a rich source of vitamin C and fibre. It is said that eating the green pawpaw helps to combat hypertension.

Passion Fruit, Granadilla: *Passiflora quadrangularis.* This fruit is contained in a brownish-purple casing which becomes crinkly when ripe. The pulp surrounding the seeds is used to make drinks, ice creams and desserts. It is an ideal addition to fruit salads. Available fresh from most greengrocers and supermarkets.

Pigeon Peas, Gunga, Arhar Dhal, Gandules: Are native to west Africa but are widely used in all cooking throughout the Caribbean. They are available canned or dried, and are used in soups, stews and rice.

Pimento, Allspice, Jamaica Pepper: *Pimenta officinalis.* A tropical tree which has small white flowers and aromatic berries (pimento) which taste like a mixture of cinnamon, cloves and nutmeg. They are bought dried in much the same way as peppercorns. Used as a flavouring in soups, stews meat and fish dishes, and to make a liqueur in Jamaica.

Plantain: *Musa paradisiaca.* A large, banana-like, tropical musaceous plant. This fruit is eaten as a vegetable either fried or boiled, and when green, it is made into chips. It is a favoured accompaniment to a number of poultry, fish and meat dishes and regularly eaten fried.

Pomelo: See Shaddock

Rum, Rhum: An alcoholic drink made from sugar cane which can be white (clear), dark brown or golden. It is produced in every country of the Caribbean, each with its own specific flavour and strength. Since colonialism, rum production has been one of the region's major industries.

Salt Cod: Also known as salt fish, bacalao and morue in the French-speaking Caribbean. Originally, it was used to feed the slaves. It was also fed to Portuguese sailors and is still one of the dishes served in Portugal. Other types of fish are salted, such as ling and mackerel, but salt cod remains the favourite. It can be purchased in specialist Caribbean, Indian and Portuguese food shops. It is now readily available, in packets or fresh, in supermarkets and fishmongers.

Saltpetre: *Sal petrae*. Potassium nitrate, a colourless or white crystalline compound, used as a food preservative, especially as a curing agent for ham, sausages and beef. Can usually be purchased in pharmacies.

Sea Moss: See Irish Moss

Seville Orange: *Citrus aurantium*. Otherwise known as the sour orange, it was introduced to the Mediterranean by the Arabs in the 10th century and is now grown in all countries that grow oranges, albeit in limited quantities. The Seville orange is principally grown for marmalade, but is also good for sauces and marinades.

Shaddock, Grapefruit: *Citrus maxima or citrus decumana*. This was named after Captain Shaddock who brought the seeds to Jamaica from the east Indies in 1696. The shaddock was a slightly less sweet forerunner of the Jamaican grapefruit, which is widely available in shops and markets, and is a rich source of vitamin C. Often used as a breakfast meal, it makes a good dessert, and is ideal as part of a fruit salad, or as the base for a sauce. The juice is, of course, good to drink on its own or mixed with other juices or alcoholic drinks.

Sorrel, Rosella, Flor de Jamaica: This tropical plant, with its fleshy red sepals, is used for making jelly and jam, and is the base of a popular Christmas drink. It is usually available fresh at Christmas time and dried throughout the rest of the year.

Sweet Potato: *Pomona batatas*. There are several varieties which are grown throughout the Caribbean region, ranging from very sweet to slightly sweet. It is served in a number of ways including desserts, cakes and as a side vegetable. The potato is rich in carbohydrates and vitamin C, and is a good source of fibre. The flesh may be orange, red or white.

Tamarind: *Tamaridus indica*. The tamarind is an extremely versatile fruit that is used in a variety of ways. Its bittersweet taste is found in curries, Angostura Bitters, Worcestershire sauce, as well as sweets, drinks, preserves and chutneys. When ripe, the pod is brown and about 5-12 cm/2-5 inches long. Tamarinds are available fresh and dried in a number of specialist shops and markets.

Tannia: See Dasheen

Tawa: Is a flat cast iron griddle used when making roti and similar breads. It can be purchased in many south Asian catering shops.

Yam: *Dioscorea* family. This root vegetable is widely used throughout the Caribbean in much the same way as the Europeans use potatoes. The large, swollen tuber, which forms the yam, has a thick brown hairy skin and the flesh is either white or yellow. Like the potato, it is always cooked before eating and is used in both sweet and savoury dishes.

Index to Recipes

Notes

Notes

Notes

Weights, Measures & Conversions

SOLIDS

Grams	Ounces
(nearest 10 g)	
10 g	½ oz
20 g	¾ oz
30 g	1 oz
60 g	2 oz
80 g	3 oz
110 g	4 oz (¼ lb)
140 g	5 oz
170 g	6 oz
200 g	7 oz
230 g	8 oz (½ lb)
250 g	9 oz
280 g	10 oz
310 g	11 oz
340 g	12 oz (¾ lb)
370 g	13 oz
400 g	14 oz
420 g	15 oz
450 g	1 lb (16 oz)
570 g	1¼ lbs
680 g	1½ lbs
900 g	2 lbs
1 kg	2¼ lbs
1.3 kg	3 lbs
1.8 kg	4 lbs
2.3 kg	5 lbs

CONVERSIONS

To convert	Multiply by
Ounces to grams	28.35
Grams to ounces	0.03527
Pounds to grams	453.6
Grams to pounds	0.002205
Pounds to kgs	0.4536
Kilograms to lbs	2.205
Pints to litres	0.568
Litres to pints	1.760
Fl oz to ml	28.4

LIQUIDS

Millilitres	Fluid Ounces
(nearest 10 ml)	
30 ml	1 fl oz
60 ml	2 fl oz
90 ml	3 fl oz
120 ml	4 fl oz
150 ml	5 fl oz (¼ pint)
180 ml	6 fl oz
210 ml	7 fl oz
240 ml	8 fl oz
270 ml	9 fl oz
300 ml	10 fl oz (½ pint)
450 ml	15 fl oz (¾ pint)
600 ml	1 pint
750 ml	1¼ pints
900 ml	1½ pints
1.2 litres	2 pints
1.4 litres	2½ pints
2.3 litres	4 pints

OVEN TEMPERATURES

Gas Mark	Fahrenheit	Centigrade
1	275°F	140°C
2	300°F	150°C
3	325°F	160°C
4	350°F	180°C
5	375°F	190°C
6	400°F	200°C
7	425°F	220°C
8	450°F	230°C
9	475°F	240°C